MONGO
ADVENTURES IN TRASH

TED BOTHA

BLOOMSBURY

Published by Bloomsbury Publishing, New York and London
Distributed to the trade by Holtzbrinck Publishers

All papers used by Bloomsbury Publishing are natural, recyclable products made
from wood grown in well-managed forests. The manufacturing processes conform
to the environmental regulations of the country of origin.

The Library of Congress has cataloged the hardcover edition as follows:

Botha, Ted.
Mongo / Ted Botha.—1st U.S. ed.
p. cm.
ISBN 1-58234-452-3 (hc)
1. Collectors and collecting—Social aspects. 2. Collectors and collecting—Social
aspects—United States. 3. Collectors and collecting—Social aspects—South
Africa. 4. Botha, Ted—Journeys—South Africa. 5. United States—Social life and
customs—20th century. 7. United States—Description and travel.
8. South Africa—Description and travel. I. Title.

AM231.B68 2004
790.1'32—dc22
2003028009

First published in the United States by Bloomsbury Publishing in 2004
This paperback edition published in 2005

Paperback ISBN 1-58234-567-8
ISBN-13 978-1-58234-567-3

1 3 5 7 9 10 8 6 4 2

Typeset by Palimpsest Book Production Limited,
Polmont, Stirlingshire, Scotland
Printed in the United States of America by Quebecor World Fairfield

For Joe

contents

mongo *n.* **1** [1970s +] (US) an idiot. **2** [1980s +] (US, New York) any discarded object that is retrieved. **3** [1980s +] (US, New York) a scrap-metal scavenger.

The Cassell Dictionary of Slang

introduction

When I was about twelve, I started collecting used batteries, double-A, triple-A, C, D, 9-volt, and even the big square kind that you had to attach wires to. They were all old and useless, but I collected them anyway and put them in a shoe box in my bedroom closet. I also collected matchboxes, Matchbox cars, empty miniature liqueur bottles, stamps, and coins. The collections all had one thing in common: They just sat in the closet, and I did absolutely nothing with them.

The shoe boxes stood side by side, neatly arranged, and were opened only every six months or so, when I briefly looked at their contents, ran my hands through the coins, then put everything back in the closet again. Maybe I amassed worthless items to compensate for some deeper problem in my life—sadness, loneliness, nerdiness—but I like to think that there was a simpler explanation. I was born to collect things.

Nothing in our home was ever thrown away if it could be recycled. Furniture got repaired, books got rebound, uneaten food was frozen and then rehashed in spaghetti or a meal for the dogs. The one excess my parents allowed themselves was antiques, although they bought only things they could get for an exceptionally good price. Their career as diplomats allowed them to do this in various parts of the world, and I can remember many a weekend spent driving along the lanes

outside Washington, D.C., Tokyo, or wherever we happened
to be living at the time, in search of unlikely places where a
bargain might be found.

Whenever we went home to South Africa, I saw how people
took recycling a step farther than our family did, while the
word *bargain* gained a whole new meaning. What was considered garbage in the countries we had just come from—discarded
wire, old Coke cans, plastic shopping bags, cardboard, and
rusty refrigerator doors—was used, often quite ingeniously, to
make toys, ornaments, houses, and even entire suburbs. No
wonder, then, that by the age of twelve, I couldn't decide what
to throw away and what to collect, the valuable or the valueless, battery or antique.

By the time I moved to New York, in the 1990s, I was more
discriminating about what I kept or discarded, but I still understood thrift and value, and I could never pass up a bargain.
When I saw the things that people were tossing onto the sidewalk as I was about to move into my first apartment, I finally
understood what my battery-collecting youth had prepared
me for: to use other people's garbage to furnish my home for
free.

With very little effort, I obtained a sofa, carpets, lamps,
paintings, potted plants, a dish rack, cutlery, and bookshelves,
as well as numerous books and a pile of fifty-year-old *New
Yorker*s to fill them with. At first convinced that I had done
something innovative and unheard-of—inspired in equal parts
by the prudence of my parents and the ingenuity of Africa—
I soon discovered that furnishing your apartment off the sidewalk has been a New York tradition for a very long time. Or
at least for as long as people have been throwing away things
that still have life in them.

Not that these particular collectors have gotten their due. They have managed to slip through the cracks of history, hardly noticed, taken more often than not for bums or lunatics. Other collectors, the *real* ones, the ones who occupy themselves with stamps and coins and airplanes, have been written about over and over again, but the collectors of things that people throw away are mere footnotes in little-known books about sewers and sanitation.

The street collector you see today could well be a bum or a lunatic, that's true enough, but just as easily a millionaire, a schoolteacher, an accountant, a doctor, a housewife. Much of the story about what they collect, and how and why, is passed along orally, like some secret religion. And perhaps because their pastime is still so easily misunderstood—"Ugh, you collect garbage?" is the refrain that usually greets them—it's seldom that they willingly declare themselves.

Only once you have acknowledged that you're a believer too are collectors happy to open up. And when they do, they blossom, like any real collector would, and their stories fascinate. Some of them also have a word for what they find, a word that is suitably playful and vague. It could be French, Chinese, or even African, but it is, quite appropriately, American slang, concocted in New York for any discarded item that is picked up, retrieved, rescued. That word is *mongo*.

It was not easy for me to discover collectors of mongo at first. They go out at odd hours and have a knack of disappearing like a phantom or a cat in the night. You hear the garbage lid rattle, but when you look for them they are gone. I started heading out myself at all hours of the day and night, and I approached anyone who displayed the distinctive characteristics, whether it was a homeless person pushing a shopping cart through traffic, a businessman in a suit heading home after work lugging a slightly damaged chair that clearly hadn't come from Ikea, or a well-dressed woman whose bag wasn't a petite Gucci but a thirty-gallon Glad. I learned at the same time how to discern the collectors from the legion of dabblers, such as the well-to-do housewife who plucked an end table off the sidewalk twenty years ago and has been living off the anecdote of her "shabby chic" ever since.

In time, I also discovered that collectors don't go only for what you see on the sidewalk but also for what lies under the sidewalk and behind the sidewalk. Sometimes they take the very sidewalk itself. I call them collectors because they choose so many different words to describe themselves. They are pickers and finders, lookers and diggers, Dumpster divers and sludgers, street farmers and urban survivalists. Many of them began collecting somewhere else—in Paris, Mexico City, the hill towns of Ecuador, the farming towns of Iowa, the retirement communities of Florida—before they landed up in New York. Some began in New York, moved away, and then came back again. Their styles of collecting differ as much as their mongo, but they all agree on one thing: New York can't be beat. The combination of wealth, residents living at close quarters, and the fact that so much gets thrown away out of lack of space, sheer laziness, ignorance, or wastefulness means there's lots of mongo and it's easy to reach. All you need to find it is a good pair of walking shoes, a shopping cart, a route, a timetable of the city's garbage-collecting days, a capacity to deal with looks that can be more severe than the smells, a willingness to go out at three in the morning or an equally inconvenient daytime hour—try dragging a desk through afternoon traffic—and, most of all, a sense of adventure.

Collecting can become addictive too, and anyone you see out there who is standing on top of a dump or in a Dumpster, tearing at a garbage bag, slicing open a box, riffling through a tied-up stack of magazines, shouldering a legless table, or inspecting old mattresses is often just as committed to his or her pursuit as any philatelist or numismatist. And if you bother to ask what they have found, you will understand why.

chapter 1

the pack rats

It is four o'clock in the morning when the phone rings. Sarah's voice sounds a lot younger than her fifty-five years, except for a huskiness that comes from having just woken up or from years of smoking too much. She says she will be in the city by five-thirty A.M., then laughs, very girl-like and enthusiastic.

"I'm on my way," she says.

Despite Sarah's promise, there is every reason not to believe her. In the past year she has repeatedly let me down. At the same time, I have grown fond of her, and I keep expecting her to prove to me what a great collector she is. Much of my faith is based on the fact that she was the first collector I met, and for a long time she remained the only one I knew.

There were plenty of people who told me they collected, but they weren't what I was looking for. None of them went out regularly. They picked up a piece of furniture here, a lamp there, and only, mind you, if they had the time and the patience to schlep it home. They were as dedicated and consistent as a vacationer gathering seashells at the shore.

There were also lots of wonderful collector stories, about someone who knew someone else who had collected something magnificent once upon a time—an armoire with a few scratches, a chaise longue done in burgundy velvet, a marble bust blackened by soot that was cleaned off in a jiffy. But when I tried to track down the objects or their finders, I got nowhere. The stories could have been true, but I wrote them off as urban legends, which proliferate in street-collecting circles.

I followed up on anyone who had the tiniest bit of potential, which led to many a protracted detour. A schoolteacher named Jack seemed like a good candidate from the moment I saw him walking down Madison Avenue one weekday afternoon with a broken chair on his shoulder. Yes, he said, he was a collector and had been doing it for five years. It took several months to organize a visit to his small beach cottage in City Island, but I was sure the wait would be worth it. As soon as I walked through his front door, though, my heart sank. I had seen better mongo on the street that morning.

Sarah, on the other hand, had come from an antiques-collecting family that was slightly eccentric, and she had collected off the street for more than thirty years, in New York, Philadelphia, and Tennessee. Once, in Manhattan, she had found a crib dating back to the Civil War period that she later sold for five hundred dollars. Moreover, she was eager to talk about it all.

"I've been wanting to write down my memories about collecting," she told me when I first approached her. "This will give me a chance. Call me."

When I called, there was no reply. I tried again numerous times after that, but it was as if she had disappeared. Six months later, she suddenly answered the phone as if she'd been there all along. She was bubbly and girlish, as eager as ever to talk about collecting.

"I've been writing down my thoughts," she said, picking up the conversation where we'd left off.

We agreed on a date to meet at her house in New Jersey, my faith in her renewed. But that didn't last, for she'd given me the wrong directions to get there. Perhaps it was an honest mistake, but perhaps she really didn't want to talk. Was this the erratic kind of behavior I could expect from all collectors? Maybe garbage wasn't something you opened up about as easily as Japanese porcelain or model cars. But when I finally got to Sarah's house, she was as warm and gushing as ever and couldn't understand what had kept me away for six months.

"You have made me think about all the years that I've been collecting," she said, addressing me like an old friend. In her garage, I admired a broken green leather armchair. "Do you like that?" she asked, one collector to another. "Oh, you must have it. I'm going to give it to you."

I mention the green armchair because it was the only piece I noticed in a garage packed so full of things that you could hardly walk in it, let alone park a car. It was the kind of stuff that didn't inspire awe but confusion, giving the place the jumbled air of a junkyard. The same went for her garden, which belonged in a trailer park and not at the end of a leafy cul-de-sac in New Jersey. My heart didn't sink exactly—I kept reminding myself that she'd once found a Civil War crib—but my confidence in her collecting abilities took a severe knock.

Inside her house, the things she'd collected were more interesting—an antique gas stove that didn't work, baskets that were hung from the ceiling, a display cabinet—but they were hardly impressive. Was this the best she could muster after three and a half decades? Even her husband, Rich, had done better, having built the entire house out of bricks he'd recovered from various demolition sites.

In the basement, Rich also had a collection of secondhand books that he sold on the Internet. As we went downstairs to see them, I was tempted to ask whether the books had also been found, but I didn't. They looked valuable, and I was sure they couldn't have been thrown out. In the coming months I would learn that they could have.

I assumed that Sarah and Rich's mutual love of amassing things was what had brought them together in the first place, but it turns out that several of the men she had been involved with in her life—Rich is her fourth husband—had been collectors. Whether or not that was a coincidence, Rich made sure to point out that even though they both collected, their collections were very different. His was a business; hers he dismissed as "cockroaches."

Sarah's routine, she told me, was to drive her Dodge Caravan through the suburbs near their home on garbage days, or simply when the urge took her. On the way home, she might also make a detour, just in case something had been thrown out unexpectedly. Certain items she would clean up—buckets, mason jars, shelves—and then decorate and sell, while others just lay there, a fact that clearly irritated Rich.

"He says, 'What are you going to do with that? What's *that* for? Where are you going to put those things?'" A mischievous look crossed her face. "I tell him, 'Honey, I'm not going to put them anywhere. I'm going to sell them.' But I don't. I have this box of wooden hangers I found seven years ago. I was going to paint them, put these flowers on them. You know the bitch of it? I haven't done a damn thing with them."

Oddly enough, though, Rich could be as much of an accomplice as a restraint. While he scorned her cockroaches, he sometimes helped her find them. Whenever he was out walking the dog and discovered something he liked, he hid it in the bushes till he could come back for it. Whenever they went vacationing in the Appalachians, where they have a cottage, they returned from the dump site with just as much as they took there to throw away. At those times, he could relate to what Sarah was doing.

"You look at an object and see hidden behind the grime this worthwhile thing," he told me. "That's part of the fun."

When I left Sarah's house that day, I asked her if she wanted to go collecting with me in the city. Despite what I'd seen at her house, I still believed in her. Maybe I'd set my sights too high to begin with, expecting her to have achieved on the street what a collector of illuminated scripts or eighteenth-century coins might have done in an antiques store. Maybe collectors of garbage didn't make the kind of jaw-dropping discoveries of other collectors.

I hoped that bringing Sarah to New York would jog her memories of collecting there thirty-five years earlier. But each time we set a date, she never showed up. We went through the same delaying tactics as before, which, I realized, had nothing to do with collecting but with Sarah. She didn't answer the phone or return my calls, but when she finally did she was brimming with excitement.

"I can't wait to come. I have started writing about collecting," she said. This time she added, "I call it my purge."

But then she backed off again. She made excuses—she was too busy, relatives were visiting, someone died—but then the truth finally came out. Rich was interfering.

"He doesn't want me bringing home any more cockroaches."

I suggested, as a compromise, that she drive to the city and we simply look at garbage, not actually pick it up. This, I suspected, was like putting a full case of Johnnie Walker in front of a recovering alcoholic, but, surprisingly, Sarah agreed.

After all the months of unfulfilled promises, the morning I receive Sarah's wake-up call I doubt that she will actually show up. I get dressed but don't bother going downstairs to wait for her. I also decide that this will be our last appointment. If she doesn't arrive, I will give up on her and start following several other collectors I have met in the intervening months. But at five-thirty A.M., I hear a car horn and look out the window. It's Sarah, small and beaming, in her Dodge Caravan.

At that very same moment, barely a mile away from us, the personnel of Manhattan Seventy are arriving at their work-place. As they saunter into the two-story building, you can see that the backs of their green overalls are emblazoned with a logo that could be mistaken for the designer Donna Karan's. But it's not DKNY, it's DSNY.

Parked in front of Manhattan Seventy are dozens of big white trucks with SANITATION written in small letters on the sides. Before they start off on their morning run, they resemble huge robotic beetles, or cockroaches even, in repose between feeding on the city's detritus. The trucks are also the only things that give away the identity of Manhattan Seventy, a dirty-brick structure that's located anonymously between two open lots not far from a highway. Inside, the depot resembles a parking garage, except there aren't any cars. On the second floor, a row of flimsily made offices line one wall, while the rest of the cavernous space is occupied by a pool table, a Ping-Pong table, an old wooden phone booth, and a couple of Police Do Not Cross This Line barriers. At the head of the stairs stands a stuffed dog, more a joke than a mascot, its one ear chewed, its moth-eaten fur covered with a DSNY sweat-shirt, and three of its paws clad in socks and two in heavy construction boots. It looks exactly like the kind of object someone might pull out of the garbage.

But it shouldn't be. Sanitation workers are not allowed to collect for themselves what they collect for the city. According to General Order No. 96–09, section 3.17 of the DSNY's Code of Conduct, "Employees may not sort through garbage. Employees may not take for their personnel [*sic*] or other than department use any material put out for collection." Members of the public are forbidden to do it too, but they're banned by a different city ordinance. The New York Administrative Code, Title 16, section 7 (b) states that "No person, other than an authorized employee or agent of the department [of sanitation] shall disturb or remove any ashes, garbage or light refuse or rubbish placed by householders, or their tenants, or by occupants or their servants, within the stoop or area line, or in front of houses or lots, for removal, unless requested by residents of such houses."

What Sarah and I are about to do, therefore, is illegal. What hundreds, maybe thousands, of collectors across New York do is illegal and punishable with a fine. Not many people seem to know this, but every single item that gets thrown away—soda can, sofa, disposable diaper, washing machine—becomes the city's property as soon as it reaches the sidewalk. I always thought that I was doing sanitation workers a favor each time I picked up something; it was one less object for them to remove. But the DSNY maintains that collectors, no matter what they're collecting, make a mess and actually *increase* the work of its employees.

Finding this out, however, was not easy. In a year of trying to reach the DSNY to get its view on collectors, all my calls were redirected or went unanswered, and my messages and faxes got lost in a black hole. Sarah at least fed me a line, gave me a bit of hope, but not the DSNY. I couldn't help concluding that the department was too embarrassed to admit that it didn't know anything about collectors or, for some reason, didn't want to talk about them.

Eventually I got two brief replies, which referred me to the abovementioned clauses, 3.17 and 7 (b), and gave me a few statistics that I already had (for example, seven hundred trucks from seventy depots go out daily to gather thirteen thousand tons of trash). Meanwhile, the spokesman who explained why collecting is forbidden refused to go into details, if there were any.

This left me with the distinct impression that the DSNY is the collector's Enemy Number 1, when it is, in many ways, the exact opposite. If it weren't for New York's recycling program, for instance, can collectors wouldn't be able to quickly iden-tify the clear plastic bags containing their kind of gold, saving them many hours of searching. If it weren't for New York's bulk-garbage days, furniture collectors wouldn't know when to go out, or which part of the city to focus their attention on. The DSNY even tries to stop garbage from being created by encouraging manufacturers to send industrial discards to various not-for-profit organizations, which find other uses for them. Why, then, would it outlaw civilians from doing exactly the same thing? Admittedly, I never once heard of someone being fined for picking something off the street, but the regulations remain in place. Meanwhile, collectors make full use of the city's sanitation schedule and the sanitation department turns a blind eye. It's a relationship that's as imperfect as it is old.

A hundred years and fifty years ago, collectors went by different names, whether it was ragpicker, chiffonier, or trimmer. They were poor and often homeless people who sought out rags, glass, metal, bones—anything that could be used again or sold for a few cents a pound. There were probably bigger items available too, for the same axiom of today must have applied back then: Great wealth makes great garbage. And New York of the late nineteenth century certainly had wealth to throw around as well as to throw out. As Charles Beard wrote in *The Rise of American Civilization*, "Diamonds were set in teeth; a private carriage and personal valet were provided for a pet monkey . . . $65,000 was spent for a dressing table, $75,000 for a pair of opera glasses." Yet in the same way that there is a queue for garbage today (be it the hired help in a Park Avenue apartment, the doormen downstairs, or even the sanitation workers), the line was probably even longer a century ago, at the very end of which stood the ragpicker.

They combed the streets, where garbage could lie for months if the private cartmen—and, after 1881, the sanitation department—didn't come to collect it, the piles gradually mixing with horse manure and mud until they were several feet high. Ragpickers also scoured the dumps along the Hudson and East rivers, where garbage accrued before being put on scows, taken onto the water, and off-loaded. What they found they then sorted, cleaned, and sold, often in a small area of the Bowery that became known as Ragpickers' Row.

The abysmal conditions of the poor were captured at the time in the photographs of Alice Austen and Jacob Riis, who tried to raise public awareness of this other side of New York.

When change eventually came to the lives of ragpickers, however, it was brought about not by a humanitarian but by a sanitarian. George Waring, who was appointed chief of sanitation in the late 1800s, introduced an almost militaristic approach to cleaning the city, and his team of white-uniformed sweepers in pith helmets patrolled the streets with brooms and newly designed buckets on wheels. He not only opened up the thoroughfares (Riis himself took a set of pictures of Morton Street before Waring, when it was covered in almost a foot of manure and refuse, and after, when it resembled a street you'd recognize today), he is also credited with having planted the seed of recycling many decades before the term was coined. In a less auspicious move, he gave the contract to gather recyclables to his brother-in-law, effectively cutting off at least part of the ragpickers' resources.

But Waring wasn't the only person changing the urban landscape and the way garbage was thought of in New York. The creators of Central Park had already started the transformation. A former boss of Waring's, a man named Egbert Vielé, had, as the city's most famous sanitation engineer, worked on the drainage of a large tract of land in the center of Manhattan before Frederick Law Olmsted designed the park, which was meant to be an escape for New Yorkers from the smells and sights of dumps, manure, and privies. Paris had done the same under Baron Haussmann, turning places like the offal-corpse-garbage dumping ground of Montfaucon, where ragpickers lived and worked, into the green-hilled Buttes-Chaumont.

The actions of Waring, Vielé, and Olmsted must have severely affected ragpicking, for by cleaning up the streets and wiping out the shantytowns and Seneca Village where the park was to go, they effectively shrank the ragpickers' collecting and living space. But the survival of collectors for the next century and a half suggests that all of this would be only a temporary setback.

Sarah is the great-niece of Frederick Law Olmsted. She tells me this as we drive through early-morning Central Park, on the way from the Upper West Side to the Upper East. I immediately try to read more into her family tree than I should. Is she some kind of link between the garbage-collecting days of old New York and today? Or am I just trying, once again, to substantiate my belief in her as a collector?

I turn my attention back to the mission at hand. We have crossed the park to reach an area where garbage is thrown out on Tuesday mornings. There is little traffic before six A.M., so Sarah can set her own pace without having to worry about a taxicab or bus rushing up behind us. That helps when we constantly have to slow down to look between parked vehicles for the telltale signs of collectibles: worn-out furniture, discarded lamps, wilting potted plants.

Sarah turns down Lexington Avenue. At each corner, we stop and look left and right to see if an apartment building or brownstone has put anything out, but there is very little. That is not unusual. Even though the sanitation trucks will get here in just over an hour's time, buildings wait until the last minute to discard refuse. They do this to discourage people from scavenging and thus—or so the belief goes—from making a mess.

"If we don't find anything," she says, "I won't be disappointed."

But I know she will be. This is an anniversary of sorts. Even though she has come back to the city occasionally to collect over the years, she hasn't done it for more than a decade.

At the end of one block, we both see something at the same

time, and Sarah instinctively accelerates. It's only cardboard, though, dozens of boxes that have been cut up and placed in such a way that they resemble something valuable at a distance, a desk or a bookcase, even. The collector's mirage.

Sarah and I both should have known better. Reading garbage from afar is something a collector learns, along with what days of the week are best to go out, which areas and buildings can be depended on, and that the end of the month is a particularly promising time, seeing as that's when people who are moving throw out belongings they normally would've kept. Sarah isn't deterred by the cardboard.

"Somebody else's cardboard box could be our treasure," she says hopefully.

The car lurches forward again. Sarah has spied something else, and this time it's more than just cardboard, but not much more. Sarah says, "Oooohhh!" and laughs nervously. But on arrival we are met by several sidewalk standards, pieces that you regularly come across but that no one ever seems to particularly want: the fixer-upper (a chair with the rattan seat worn through), the oddity (an aquarium), the questionable (a vacuum cleaner, a futon), or the marginal (crutches, a baby stroller). Sarah considers the aquarium, more because she wants to find something than because she needs it.

"What am I going to do with an aquarium?" she asks out loud.

She does this several times throughout the morning, carrying on a little debate that she's clearly had with herself many times before. *Should I take it? No, rather not. Maybe I could find some use for it. But where?* Yes-no-yes-no. It's as if she were shopping for an article of clothing that she knows her closet is already full of.

As we continue our fitful drive, stop-start-stop-start, yes-no-yes-no, Sarah at last starts reminiscing about the past, when New York was a collector's paradise. It was the late 1960s when she eloped with her first husband, Gary, and they moved from New Jersey to a small apartment in New York's East Village, which was the center of a thriving counterculture. The streets, parks, and coffee shops were full of bohemians and transients. Artists found their supplies on the sidewalk, turning wood, metal, old bicycle wheels, and frames into sculptures, while hippies found things they could sell to buy their next fix or joint. A decade later, antiques dealers would cotton on to what was being thrown away, and a decade after that, Martha Stewart would announce that the old-and-crusty look was recherché, causing people to be more prudent about what they threw out. But the 1960s was the golden age.

"There was so much on the street back then," Sarah recalls, slowing down near a pile of garbage on Park Avenue. "And it was good stuff. No one seemed to have any idea of antiques. But I did. I was brought up with antiques around me, so I knew what things were worth. When a building was demolished, everything would be thrown out. Oh, I remember these wonderful wooden mantelpieces."

Like most people, the newlyweds Sarah and Gary were motivated by an empty apartment and no money with which to furnish it. They had a friend with a van, another with a taxi, and they would drive around the city looking for things they could throw in the back and take home: bolts of material from the Garment District she would use to cover cushions and make curtains, heavy mahogany furniture from churches, iron gates that Sarah put in their garden.

"It became like an addiction. I always had to go out when I knew there was a garbage collection. Once you start, you have to go out. There's this fear that you might miss something."

Sometimes they collected with a group of hippies. Their big collecting day was Saturday, and afterward they would drink coffee or have lunch in Tompkins Square Park. A friend of Sarah's in San Francisco told her that they followed exactly the same collecting routine in Haight-Ashbury.

"I knew the garbagemen better than the people who were collecting with me, but we were all into the same thing. Garbage. Elegant junk. Still, there was a camaraderie. The suburbs don't have that."

Sarah got to know people—children who played on the street, gang members who told her they could protect her only if she stayed on their block—because of her collecting forays. Her fellow collectors, meanwhile, she often knew not by name but by style. The greedy grabbers, the finicky pickers, the deliberate lookers, the old Italian woman with a shopping cart who would go through everything, talking to herself about what she could do with something or other, and then leaving empty-handed.

After a year, Sarah left Gary and New York, moving to rural Tennessee with her new boyfriend Bobby. She kept on collecting, even though the terrain and the collectibles changed dramatically. Not far from where Bobby's parents owned a honky-tonk, the Tennessee Valley Authority was preparing to flood the Little Tennessee River to make way for the Tellico Dam, and residents had already been moved out of their homes. When Sarah and Bobby drove through the area, they came across mansions where furniture, trunks, and clothes had simply been left behind.

"It was like the people had just closed the doors and never come back," she remembers. "It was so weird."

Each time Sarah went out collecting, no matter where she was, she would make up a story about what she found. This act of make-believe had become part of her routine during her time in the East Village. She wondered whose hand had turned this porcelain door handle or who had sat on that chair. "There was this sense that these things had been around for so long," she says. Walter Benjamin once wrote that "for a true collector the whole background of an item adds up to a magic encyclopedia whose quintessence is the fate of his object." This background could include its origin, its date of manufacture, its creator, or its last owner, but Sarah always added a fifth element to the scenario: herself.

In her stories, she was the daughter of a domestic servant and had to shovel the front walk. She would go out collecting for her family, getting a pot for her mother, a shelf for her father. In truth, she came from a well-to-do family and her father had died in an accident when she was only three. But the stories she told herself, like the collecting, were a means of escape from a life that wasn't always pleasant and sometimes got violent. She had run away from a home she actually liked in order to follow Gary, and now that the marriage had gone bad she didn't know how to go back without losing face. In Tennessee, she lived in a trailer with Bobby, who was still married to someone else, and he would get drunk and beat her.

"Collecting was good for me," she says, hugging the steering wheel, which she can barely see over. "I still tell that story. That's part of the lure of collecting. I play a game."

* * *

Nelson makes up different kinds of stories—actually, you could call them theories—about what he collects. For instance, there's the one about how valuable objects get thrown away by people who don't have very much money to begin with.

"What happens," he once told me, "is the mother passes away, and the kids just want to take the money and whatever is in the house. The rest goes. You open these bags and there's old antique glasses, cups, paintings. I know how many bags should be outside a building, so when I see more than usual, I know someone has died and stuff has been thrown out."

Nelson works at Manhattan Seventy, the sanitation depot with the stuffed dog mascot. The fact that he also collects mongo took me as long to find out as it did to get some answers out of the DSNY. Sanitation workers on the whole won't talk about collecting for a very different reason from their employer. They aren't supposed to collect, but many of them do. Before meeting Nelson, I had seen sanitation workers rescue items from the trash numerous times. Even as Sarah and I are driving around, we get stuck behind a sanitation truck whose driver picks up a chair, takes it around to a compartment behind his cab, and stores it there before driving on.

Every time I asked sanitation workers about collecting, however, they played dumb. *Collect, us?* If there were great things to be found on New York's sidewalks, they hadn't noticed and they certainly didn't do it themselves. Once or twice one of them let slip that a colleague collected and then sold the stuff on weekends, but whenever I tried to get details, they somehow couldn't remember. How, I wondered, did something as valueless as garbage suddenly become so valuable that no one wanted to talk about it?

I had almost given up on the sanitation workers when I met Nelson, who happened to work on my street. I'd been looking all over the city for someone like him when all along he had been at my doorstep three times a week. He called himself the King of Collectors, although the bandanna he wore around his head when he worked made him look, quite fittingly, like a pirate. He said he had started collecting twenty years ago, when his first job was on and around Delancey Street, and he noticed his partner doing it.

"He didn't care what it was he took, and then he sold it. He'd say, 'This is worth fifty cents to somebody.' He took everything—fish tanks, records, pictures, whatever was worth something."

Nelson stores his collection in the heart of Manhattan Seventy. The day I went to see it, he met me on the drab second floor, near the stuffed dog, then led the way into the men's locker room. As soon as we passed through the door, the lifeless, dim warehouse exploded with light and color, all because of what Nelson has found. Plants were hung from the ceiling and the fifteen-foot-high walls were covered in paintings and posters. They lay in rows four deep, about two hundred in all, giving the locker room the feeling more of a gallery than a place where garbagemen changed out of their dirty overalls. The posters, all of them framed, ran the gamut from James Dean to the rock group Social Distortion, from *Atlantic Monthly* covers to exhibitions of Matisse and Chagall at the Galerie Maeght in Paris, from cabaret shows to old movies like Judy Garland's *A Star Is Born* and John Huston's *L'Odyssée de l'African Queen*. The paintings included over-ripe sunsets in Puerto Rico and windblown dunes in the Sahara, portraits and landscapes, animals and sailboats, and, almost unnoticeable between them, several oils that looked quite valuable—a 1940s New York street scene, a Mediterranean village painted in 1952, and a New England lighthouse. The only subject you won't find is a nude, for, as Nelson explained, hanging a nude is against DSNY rules.

Below the artwork, men sat at a table playing cards while others who were shirtless bathed themselves at a large antique basin. Most of the men not only know where Nelson's collection comes from—as if there could be any doubt—but also regularly inquire after his latest finds.

"They ask me, 'You got any good mongo today?' or 'Let's see your mongo.' And me, I say, 'Yeah, I've done some good mongo picking. Real good.'"

Nelson sometimes splits what he collects with his partner, who usually is interested only in jewelry. If they find gold, whoever likes it takes it, and if neither one likes it, they sell it and share the money. The twenty diamonds in a ring they found on the Upper West Side, for instance, went into his partner's medallion, while its gold fetched two hundred dollars. Despite all the fairness, though, it's Nelson who normally finds the jewelry, because he seems to have a sixth sense.

"I just *feel* that something is in the bag," he said. "I know it. My partner once took a bag and put it in the truck. I heard something and went and opened it. I found silver rings, all with the markings on them, and chains." He laughed. "Yeah, I heard something. That's what they say here, I can hear it."

Nelson led me to a corner of the huge locker room and a small cabin that he built sixteen years ago. (Many months after I saw it for the first time, I would meet a sanitation worker from another part of the city who confessed that he had heard about Nelson and his cabin, which he called "the shrine.") Small, maybe ten feet by six, the shrine was squeezed into a space between two tall windows. Near its single door was a small jungle of plants, including both fake ivies and real ficus, arranged in an imposing four-foot-wide circular bird-bath, all of which were soaked in sunlight streaming through the window. Around it and on the windowsill was an array of items too big for the shrine: four-foot Ionic columns, a crudely made bust of a man's head, a statue of the Virgin Mary, an African carving, a coconut monkey, a piece of drift-wood, a cactus, and a series of sculptures that Nelson had picked up at various times outside the same building, thrown out, he suspected, by an artist who was experimenting or was dissatisfied with his latest work.

When Nelson opened the door to the shrine, which was bolted, he did so very carefully, as if we were about to enter a sanctuary. We had to go in slowly because the room was jam-packed, the exact opposite of his spacious walls. The shrine was roofless, so once inside you could see the highest paint-ings on the outer walls. Every inch was taken up by some-thing hanging from a beam, squeezed onto a ledge, or nailed to a wall. Imagine every memento, toy, keepsake, token, souvenir you've ever owned thrown out on the street—lying near a garbage bag or on top of it, peering over the edge of a bin where it was cast unthinkingly—then multiply that number by several thousand, and you would get close to what's in the shrine. Even Nelson's brief department-store-type description didn't begin to capture the extent of his collection.

"Got crystal over there, glass over there, brass over there, china up there, watches all over the place, Beanie Babies, dolls hanging all over, toy cars, glasses, old stuff, new stuff."

He turned on four or five miniature Christmas carousels

and Nativity sets, their tunes clashing, so that "Hark, the Herald Angels Sing" ran into "Rudolph the Red-nose Reindeer" and "It Came upon a Midnight Clear," before they played all over again. Their chorus was joined by several mounted fish that, at the flick of a switch, puffed out, swished their tails, and then crooned.

Toys took up most of the space, some still unwrapped. Furbies, hundreds of yo-yos, small dinosaurs encased in Superballs, dolls spread over a small sofa that was tucked behind some shelves which were full of Pez containers, Cabbage Patch dolls, trolls, mobiles, trinkets that fast-food chains might have included with a child's order of cheeseburger and fries, including statuettes of the *101 Dalmatians*, Pinocchio pencil sharpeners, *Howdy Doody* lunch boxes, and Snoopy bobble heads. More than a shrine, it was a memorial to all the fads, crazes, Edsel-type knickknacks, Disney promotions, and Burger King giveaways of the last thirty years.

Between the toys were the ephemera, arranged in groups: sunglasses; miniature teapots; watches hanging from a long shelf; a wall of buttons (in support of, among others, Babe Ruth, the city councilor Olga Mendez, Jesse Jackson, the Reverend Sun Young Moon, and Richard Nixon); car license plates; store signs; dinner plates; silver cups; old miniature Pabst beer bottles; a box of pewter medallions commemorating Theodosius Patriarch Alexi II of the Russian Orthodox Church; coins in bottles or neatly packed in rolls; silverware; framed *Playbill* magazines; a fireplace set; mugs, some with signatures of famous people, most without; old postcards from Spain done with a blindman's stitch; jewelry boxes with dancing ballerinas on top; and an Elvis Presley tie pin.

"I've even got stuff in the refrigerator that I can't fit anywhere else," Nelson said, then went over to a white Kelvinator, which was also found on the street, and opened the door to reveal another section. Mostly there were boxed sets of Barbie dolls, all of them unopened, and he picked up several and read the dates off of them. "I look at the dates on things to find out how old they are, but I'm really not into selling the stuff. I just like to save it, find it, hang it up, and look at it."

Downstairs in Manhattan Seventy is another room of about the same size as the shrine, where Nelson stores the mongo when it first comes in and then sorts through it whenever he has a chance. When he showed it to me, it was also packed to the ceiling, but nothing was in order yet. Boxes of records lay alongside a tool chest bursting with playthings. On the floor were three brass cigarette ashtrays from an old movie house, all filled with sand, and several fax machines. Numerous bookcases were crammed with dozens of videos and CDs still in their cases, plastic pumpkins from Halloween, a set of dinner plates with the American flag on them, at least six Polaroid cameras, lamps, empty coffee-cake tins, old post-cards, new postcards, rows of books, and copies of obscure magazines like *Afghanistan in Pictures* and *Soviet Union Today*. The only items Nelson pointed out, and for no other reason than he believed they might have some kind of value, were pamphlets from the fortieth birthday, in 1984, of political radical Angela Davis and an old forty-five record from 1919.

"This says it's an original Edison recording," he said, holding up the record. "And it's in the original cover. Now, I could never throw that out."

At that moment I realized that Nelson couldn't be in a worse profession, or a better one, depending on how you looked at it: the garbage collector who can't stand to see anything thrown away. Even he admitted that if he sees something and he can fit it into the truck, he'll take it. That very morning he had come across a curtain rod—just an ordinary curtain rod, thick, wooden, about ten feet long, with two round knobs on each end—that he didn't want to see destroyed. But he couldn't squeeze it into the storage area up front.

"In the end, I just threw it in the truck, broke it up, and died looking at it."

By the time Nelson has been on his route for an hour, Sarah has retrieved a basket with a broken handle, a lazy Susan that somehow looks incomplete, a plain bench, and a small wooden ladder with brass ends that gets her ecstatic.

"You just don't find these today."

More garbage has been put out by now, and the pickings are better, but the traffic has also started building up, making it harder to pull over. Still, Sarah doesn't hesitate to stop if something catches her eye, although she draws the line at black garbage bags. She hasn't opened one since her days in Tennessee.

"I had a friend, T-Bird, who fixed cars and looked for parts in black bags. One day he told me he'd opened a bag and found a whole bunch of tampons and used Pampers. He wasn't even wearing gloves! That was it for me."

Suddenly, as if there were a conspiracy among garbage dispensers (that is, doormen and janitors) to demoralize collectors, piles of garbage start materializing at the same time as the sanitation trucks arrive to pick them up. An hour ago we were too early, but now, by seven A.M., we are too late. At least the DSNY spokesman would be happy about how little opportunity there is to mess.

As we turn a corner, we see two sanitation workers putting a white wooden stand into the crusher at the back of their truck. Sarah cries out, as if she's been wounded.

"Aaaaaah. That would've looked beautiful painted and with some flowers on it. I could have sold it for seventy bucks."

For the rest of the morning she keeps mentioning the stand, like someone who regrets not having bought something that caught their eye at an antiques store. Her regret seems totally out of proportion with the object she's missed.

"It's always like that," she explains. "You keep thinking back to the thing you missed. Why am I not satisfied? I am worried about one little piece. That's really not fair, especially when I have all this wonderful stuff."

If Nelson had been the sanitation worker on that block, Sarah probably would have gotten her shelf, for he always makes sure to leave the most salvageable things out until last. One day he saw a man and a woman who both wanted a desk that he'd put to one side, but the woman managed to get it onto her car's roof single-handedly before the man could even flag down a taxi to help him. It was the kind of demand for mongo that Nelson loves to see, although it doesn't take place that often. Sarah agrees, and she comments on how surprisingly few collectors are out. The streets of the Village in the 1960s, at least as far as she remembers, would have been crawling with grabbers and pickers and lookers.

Sarah and Nelson, I realize, have a lot in common, even though the one is a professional garbageman and the other a suburban housewife. They represent the more general collector of mongo, who doesn't go for anything in particular, doesn't need to collect, and isn't deterred by a bad day on the street. They are unwavering in their enthusiasm, undemanding, don't specialize in anything, and don't know when to say no. They have been around since the ragpickers and always will be. Their mantra could be "Collect because it's there." They get excited about seeing something as ordinary as a shelf or a curtain rod and can't wait to get home to peruse the things that they have collected. Nelson conducts the same inner debate as Sarah—should I take it? should I leave it?—and he's been doing it from the very start, two decades ago, when he came upon a cup and saucer on Delancey Street.

"I said to myself, I need it. No, throw it away. But I never saw anything like it. In the end I took it, and I was hooked."

They both use the word *treasure*—she keeps repeating some form of the cliché that someone else's cardboard or junk could be her treasure, while he calls his finds "treasures from the trash"—although what they find is anything but. The best Sarah has done is the Civil War crib, which, I discover during our drive, was only a reproduction worth two hundred dollars, not five hundred, while out of the thousands of things Nelson has, he knows what only four of them are worth. He had them appraised when an *Antiques Roadshow*–type program from PAX TV, *Treasures in Your Home*, came to town. There was a clarinet in its case ($350), a 1903 artillery shell with a general carved into the side ($450), a small oil of a nude in a gilt frame ($200), and a reproduction of a Nicholas Austi violin ($65). As for all the paintings on the locker room walls and everything in his shrine, they could be worth a fortune or nothing at all.

"One day when I retire, I'll read up about them," he told

me at the end of my visit to Manhattan Seventy. "Maybe I'll open up a store with it all."

Nelson and Sarah also turned out to be the most difficult collectors of all to find and then talk to. I don't know whether my own ability to track down collectors was honed by those months spent on the first two, or whether it was coincidence, but after them I would quickly start to amass my own collection.

Sarah and I drive for another half hour before we decide that the cockroachlike sanitation trucks have us beaten. As we head back across town, the piles of garbage become more erratic and less attractive, although we do catch sight of something that might have potential—a Dumpster. In most parts of the country, Dumpsters fulfill the role of sidewalks in New York, with location likewise being the ever-important factor, except instead of near a brownstone or an apartment building, it will be near a strip mall or along Main Street in a small town in Florida. The mongo found there, as has been listed by collectors writing to a Dumpster-diving Web site, might be a stuffed horse (outside a taxidermist), a bag full of hair and a barber's chair (a hairdresser), a hundred disposable vaginal specula (a hospital), thousands of brand-name packets of makeup (a Rite Aid drugstore), a coffin and formaldehyde (a cemetery), or a .22 rifle and nine hundred dollars in cash (along an open road somewhere).

In New York, Dumpsters are more likely to contain the leftovers of a renovation: ripped-out walls, floors, and cupboards, and occasionally the things that were inside them. Once Sarah and I climb up the side of the Dumpster and peer into it, we see that the contents lie eight feet deep, and unless we spend hours emptying it, we can consider only the topmost layer. On offer are rusted bicycles, half-used cans of paint, broken picture frames, empty liqueur bottles, exercise machines in dubious condition, and baskets. Sarah takes a tricycle ("I can use this in a garden display") and a small table ("I can paint this"). Then she digs down and pries loose a box of old photographs.

"Oh, my God!" she cries out. Once again her reaction exaggerates the significance of the discovery. "This is someone's life. How could they throw it away?"

The photos are black and white or faded color: several girls on a beach, a wedding, a Miami nightclub, a group of women from the 1960s done up like Jacqueline Susann and all hanging on to a tanned bald man in his seventies ("Man counting his blessings," it's signed on the back. "For darling Doreen, who is foremost among them, Sy"). Sarah can't control her excitement.

"This is gold!"

Really? Or is it cockroaches? You can hear the doubt creeping into her voice the longer she looks at the photographs, and, like clockwork, the inner debate begins.

"I'm going to take these," she decides, then changes her mind. "But I don't know what the hell for. No, I'm not going to take them." But maybe she should. "Now, what could I do with them? I couldn't really do anything with them." She tries again. "But if you find a really old neat one . . ."

Yes-no-yes-no.

In the end, Sarah takes the photographs and the tricycle but dumps the table that she was going to paint. As we drive away, she looks over her shoulder at the morning's haul in the back of her car. Besides the photos and the tricycle, there's the ladder, the lazy Susan, the basket, the bench, and a kerosene lamp. It doesn't look like much, but

mongo

Sarah is giggling in delight. After thirty-five years, her demands are still small.

"I'm happy," she says.

chapter 2

the survivalists

Throughout the morning, Sarah and I have passed several men with shopping carts wending their way through the traffic. One even has a laundry cart, another a baby stroller. They are collectors too, part of a community that I have gotten to know better during the long months spent waiting for Sarah and the DSNY. Going from the contents of their meager vehicles, which Sarah carefully maneuvers around, the men aren't after the same thing she is, but soda cans, random articles of clothing, milk crates, and broomsticks. Sometimes shoes are tied to the shopping cart's handles like a pair of toy dice to a car mirror.

One cart in particular is parked to the side of Fifth Avenue, its owner temporarily absent. It is piled so high with huge blue plastic bags that are filled to bursting that I'm sure it's about to topple over. With so much cargo, the cart could easily belong to a man named Mr. Murphy, but, considering the hour and the location, it's unlikely. At eight A.M., he would normally be making his way across Central Park to Ninth Avenue and then heading south to a redemption center called Wecan.

Mr. Murphy collects cans—or, as he puts it, he cans. He collects almost entirely from one place, an outdoor concert venue in Central Park called SummerStage, and he does it only during the summer, when the venue is open. The other nine months of the year he works with the homeless and people who have AIDS.

"I'm what you call a sunshine canner," he says, making it sound quite pleasant, even festive.

He has earned as little as eight dollars a day from the SummerStage cans, and as much as six hundred and fifty dollars, which, at a nickel apiece, would have amounted to thirteen thousand cans. I quickly calculate that if he can get twenty-one bags (that's just over five thousand cans) on his cart at a time, which is the most he's ever managed, his biggest haul would have required him to make a total of three trips through Central Park and down Ninth Avenue to Wecan.

"On a good day it takes forty minutes to get there, depending on the load, the traffic, the potholes on the sidewalk," he says. The more bags he has, the more careful he has to be about the condition of the roads. "It's a real balancing act."

This summer, Mr. Murphy will make about ten thousand dollars. Ordinarily he makes fifteen thousand, but SummerStage has started selling beer by the keg instead of by the can. So every time a lever gets pulled instead of a flip top, he loses five cents. In the economy of the canner, a change that a consumer wouldn't even notice will impact his earnings as severely as the cold weather, when people drink less.

"It hurts," Mr. Murphy says about the decision to use kegs, although he isn't complaining. "It's the nature of the business. In the end, they make money, I make money, and I have more than I woke up with this morning."

Not all canners are as pragmatic as Mr. Murphy. Or as friendly and open. Many of them were unwilling to talk to me about canning, or about anything at all, for that matter. Characteristically, they screamed at me or ran away, making them appear quite crazy. In many cases, according to Mr. Murphy, they probably are.

"The longer you stay on the street, the more imbalanced you become," he says. "I can meet a canner a year from now, and I can see the difference."

Mr. Murphy has been canning for ten years, four of those in Central Park. He has what he calls "the contract" for SummerStage, which makes the job sound more official than it really is. He has a verbal agreement that requires him to clean up the refreshment areas after the concertgoers have left and to remove the already bagged cans by the next morning. That's not hard work for five thousand dollars a month, a healthy salary in many a New Yorker's terms, and Mr. Murphy knows it. SummerStage is one of the best places in the city to collect high volumes at one time. It's the kind of gig that every canner wants. Large apartment buildings are also good, but a concert venue is even better. Mr. Murphy still walks the streets on the days when there isn't a concert scheduled, doing buildings and delis, but that's a different kind of work. It's harder and you need a route, which takes time to develop. SummerStage, by contrast, is one-stop canning.

Before Mr. Murphy began collecting, he worked as a dispatcher in charge of a fleet of bicycle messengers. Some of the messengers he supervised were homeless, and he talked to them frequently about their experiences of living on the street. Five years before he actually quit his job, he decided to join them and make himself homeless too. He did it for two reasons: First, he knew that he could, thanks to the tips he'd picked up at work; and second, he wanted more money to buy drugs.

"It didn't make sense to pay rent when I wanted to get high," he says.

The tradition of collecting off the street to buy narcotics or alcohol was already well established by the time Sarah arrived in the East Village in the 1960s, and it carries on today. A large percentage of the people who collect for that purpose are homeless and—as Mr. Murphy claims and, I will later find out, is indeed true—are mentally disturbed. Collecting has become an integral part of their lives, allowing them to live on the street and buy their drug of choice, thereby making it the key element in an unfortunate trinity.

"A lot of addicts start collecting because of their addiction," one former collector-addict told me. He described a simple routine that is regularly followed: You search for something in the garbage, sell it for a few dollars, score, get high, then get back to searching again. It struck me as strangely admirable that collectors who earned their money this way never resorted to crime to feed their habit, which would have been a lot easier and certainly quicker.

"Even the police know that these guys are okay," one collector told me. "There will be a police block for a crime, but they won't stop canners. They know that they don't have time for crime when they're out gathering cans at a nickel apiece."

I am curious to know if Mr. Murphy still uses drugs, but it seems indiscreet to ask, not to mention an abuse of his rare hospitality. Either way, he remains one of the best at what he does, something he has achieved by being more calculating and farsighted than most other canners from the moment he joined their ranks. At first he used the street only for sleeping, not for collecting. But he eventually couldn't take working in an office any longer, and he was convinced that he could earn as much money outdoors as indoors. And he was right. Five years of sleeping on the street had prepared him well, and in no time he had worked out a route for himself, going from apartment building to deli to garbage can. But he was always on the lookout for a better deal.

"Before I do a hustle, I observe it and I network," he says. "I get a whole lot of opinions down the line and I'll see how I can improve on the hustle to make my effort less and my profit more."

His first big hustle was Penn Station. He figured out that if he could get onto the Amtrak trains as they arrived in the station, he could gather a lot of cans at once. Soon he was making up to a hundred dollars in four hours. He became a regular at the station, and so convinced were employees that he was one of them that he managed to obtain a uniform and he ate with the other workers. But after six months he was unmasked and had to move on.

Once again on the lookout for a good hustle, Mr. Murphy didn't exactly chance upon SummerStage. Like anyone who has slept in Central Park in summer, he knew about the venue and what a great source it was for cans. But somehow it eluded him until the day he and another canner went there to try to get some free food. Mr. Murphy immediately lost his appetite when his eyes fell on the huge bags of cans gathering behind the refreshment stand. He started asking around and found out that there was already someone canning there, or, as he says, who had "the contract." But Mr. Murphy managed to talk his way into getting half of it, and a year later he had it all.

How Mr. Murphy persuaded his predecessor to give up 50 percent of such a lucrative site, and then the whole thing, is kept deliberately vague. And I can't help but think that the changeover didn't take place without incident, and maybe even violently too. But the canner's world is one where you live by your wits, and from day to day, which is why some of them call themselves not redeemers, the more accepted term for canners, but professional outdoorsmen and even urban survivalists. The instability of the lifestyle—you have SummerStage today and then you lose it—also makes its participants extremely selfish.

"It's all about me and gimme," says Mr. Murphy. "Those are the two best friends anyone out here has."

If that isn't exactly the kind of behavior he admires—"I try and look further than that"—he completely understands why it occurs. Canners can be arrested for sleeping in the wrong place, or their possessions might be stolen by another canner if they leave them unattended. As a result their collections extend to much more than just cans, all of which they stash in numerous locations around the city—in bushes, under manhole covers, inside free newspaper stands, on construction sites—so that if they get arrested or robbed, they can go to their next stash and start all over.

"That's why people will walk around with carts running over with stuff," Mr. Murphy says. "You'll think, this is junk, but to them it's valuable. It's all they have."

Unlike Mr. Murphy, the vast majority of canners don't have a concert venue or even a luxury apartment building to rely on for their supply. They don't make ten thousand dollars in three years, let alone in three months. They go from trash can to trash can, sometimes gathering in a day not thousands of cans or even hundreds but only dozens. Yet in the hierarchy of street collectors, they aren't the lowliest. That position is held by anyone who goes for a black garbage bag.

"They are the lumpen proletariat of recycling," is how one collector describes them.

It's quite possible that a black-bag person could make more money than a canner, especially if something of value is discovered in the bag—a lost watch, a wedding ring that slipped off a soapy finger, a wallet that is thrown out by mistake with yesterday's newspaper. Nonetheless, the black bag itself is seen as a last resort, the recourse of anyone who doesn't care what it is he finds inside, even if, as Sarah's friend T-Bird discovered, it's old tampons and filthy diapers.

The calling card of any black-bag person can be found all over the city's sidewalks: ripped-apart bags and scattered garbage. The level of desperation invariably equals the size of the mess, which other collectors, in turn, get blamed for. If the black-bag people find something they think is valuable, they will quickly set up shop on any sidewalk and at any time of the day or night, depending on where they are less likely to be chased away by the police. After midnight on Lexington Avenue and Eighty-sixth Street, for example, a group of black-bag people regularly deal with a clientele that consists mostly of taxi drivers taking a break between late-night fares. During the day, a popular retreat is under the railway line crossing 125th Street in Harlem.

The day I wander along 125th Street the black-bag merchandise is sometimes neatly arranged on a sheet of cardboard—tired blue jeans, caseless porn videos, creased shoes, incomplete sets of fake jewelry—but just as often it is cast in a pile. It looks as if someone threw it just short of the trash can, an impression that is heightened by the absence of any sellers. The guy at the end of the block could be keeping an eye on things, but then again, perhaps the black-bag people work on an honor system, convinced that no one who is prepared to pay for garbage would steal it.

Above the black-bag people and the canners in the hierarchy are as many different collectors as there are things to collect and ways of collecting them. The old man taking a stroll down Broadway every Sunday is actually checking the pay phones for change. The Mexican with the battered pickup is after old mattresses he can sell at five dollars apiece to a company in the Bronx that recovers them, stains and all, to sell again. The guy gathering magazines will burn off the subscription labels and sell them back to news agents. The graphic artist in Chelsea selects only products with a good pedigree, whether it's a Gio Ponti chair or a bubble lamp by George Nelson. The homeless man in the Dumpster finds women's old underwear, which he sells for five dollars a pair to a businessman who likes sniffing them. His companion tears the backs off computers to get at the tiny bits of copper and gold inside. And the man driving the van with JOEL'S OLDE ANTIQUES written on its side is picking up furniture that he can sell at flea markets.

Of all these collectors, the only one I never see in action is the man with the van. Collectors in vehicles are at once the most difficult to discern—they could be mistaken for movers or dealers picking up something they bought—and the most rarefied. Because they can rescue items too big for a trolley or a shopping cart, they are also meant to hold the top position in the collector hierarchy. I often used to imagine, as I was walking or cycling around in search of collectors, that the perfect operation would be to have two people working in unison: One would be on a bicycle with a cell phone, scouring the streets, the other in a van parked somewhere in the vicinity, ready to pick things up as soon as he got a call.

Not able to find these top-end collectors on the street, I go in search of them one Sunday morning at the Twenty-sixth Street flea market, the city's biggest. I still have three blocks to go when I already spy the first telltale signs of mongo— junk spread on the pavement by a dozen black-bag guys. It is obvious that they are taking advantage of the bargain shoppers heading for the market, although they make sure (or are perhaps forced) to keep their distance. Twenty-sixth Street serves as the unofficial boundary between them and their competitors. To the south are the dealers who get to market on foot, pushing a trolley, and then set up on the sidewalk. To the north, they arrive by pickup or van and then set up under umbrellas in a fenced-off area, part of which costs a dollar to enter.

The variety on offer in the market is endless and quite overwhelming: Eastern fabrics and magazines wrapped in plastic, an old U.S. stamp dispenser and used cell phones, mannequin heads and a Dr Pepper billboard, new African art and old sewing machines, a box of old *Penthouse* magazines and tables of even older books, rusted cameras and old camera equipment, brass doorknockers and paste jewelry, frames with pictures and frames without, a five-foot statue of Jesus and a four-foot statue of an elephant, used tools and shutters, a preacher's lectern, a fox stole, two glass block side tables, Chinese porcelain, handbags, silver cutlery, khaki pants, tapestries of flowers, birdcages, suitcases, and mounds of plastic dolls. There is also plenty of furniture— new (at least as far as I can tell), 1960s, garden, Chinese, art deco.

Down Twenty-sixth Street, satellite markets have sprung up in garages and parking lots, which is where I first start noticing goods that, even though they're displayed on a table, might just as well be scattered on a sidewalk several blocks south. The dealers don't even try to hide the questionable origin of what they're selling behind a veneer of neatness. At this moment, the dividing line between antique, collectible, junk, and garbage grows vaguer than ever; or rather, it becomes clear to me that every single item at the market (or on any table or any sidewalk in the city, for that matter) could fall into any one of the four categories. Things that look like trash probably are, while things that don't look like trash could be. The problem is finding out. How do you ask someone whether what they're demanding good money for is garbage?

To my surprise, everyone I put this question to admits quite readily that lots of dealers at the market do indeed collect from the garbage. But they don't do it themselves, you under-stand. Just like the sanitation workers, most of them won't acknowledge actually doing it. I finally get pointed in the direc-tion of the one-dollar section and a woman there who sells vintage linen. As soon as I put my question to her, she raises an eyebrow, although it's not because of what I have asked but how I asked it.

"Collector?" she says, as if I have insulted her by using a word much too common for what she does. "I'm not a collector. I'm a picker." Then she proudly explains that most of her linen is thrown out by the residents of Greenwich, Connecticut. At first I find this hard to believe, especially after seeing how beautifully clean and immaculately folded everything is in her shelves. The woman notices my surprise.

"Oh, this is nothing," she says. "Look at Marge's things." She points to the stall next to hers, which is full of gilt mirrors and a small settee and several oil paintings, all cleverly arranged and very appealing. "She also picks. That's all found stuff," she says, then raises her voice. "The street is best. Right, Marge?"

The linen woman's voice is too loud, and Marge shoots her a dirty look.

"You want all these people to *know* where it comes from?" Marge says, then turns away.

The linen woman realizes her mistake. She has given away vital information; namely, the fact that she is selling for tens of dollars, even hundreds, what she got for nothing. There will be many times with collectors when I can't help wonder why they are willing to tell me about the origin of their mongo. I'm always elated when they do, but it seems like a form of self-extinction. Unlike canners, who go for a very obvious item that is available on any street corner and that no one else besides another canner wants, many collectors set their sights on the unusual and look for it in places you'd never think of. Such as linen from the leafy lanes of Greenwich. By telling me, they are alerting other would-be collectors to their mongo. They might as well be giving away a map to their secret treasure.

When the Twenty-sixth Street flea market closes for the day, there's a collectors' free-for-all. Dealers often leave behind items that they don't want to schlep home, so the same sofa or chest of drawers you would have had to pay for an hour earlier is now up for grabs. If the dealer got it off the street in the first place, he's losing nothing.

As the market empties of dealers and shoppers, clearing the way for mongo collectors to pick through the leftovers, several canners arrive too, and they make their way from trash can to trash can. An all-day market, where plenty of sodas have been consumed, is the kind of place they like. A few of the black-bag guys who have put away their wares snag a few cans as well, although they shouldn't. By doing so they are breaking one of the two basic rules that canners follow. More or less. The first: If you collect something else besides cans, you shouldn't be canning. The second: If you have been canning at a building consistently for a substantial length of time—let's say six months, seeing the period depends a lot on whom you talk to—then it's yours. Call it their version of Mr. Murphy's "contract."

One particularly large apartment building on Park Avenue belongs to Eddie, who has been doing it for two years. In some circles Eddie is known as the Soda Can King, even though he doesn't earn as much as Mr. Murphy and works longer hours and year-round. Canning for him is a full-time job. His route covers an area uptown that is several square miles in extent. At some apartment buildings he arrives early, fifteen minutes or half an hour before the cans are put out, just to be sure that no one pinches them before he can get there.

As we stand outside the Park Avenue building at sunrise one weekday, waiting for the cans to appear, Eddie notices another canner walk slowly down the street. It's clear from the meager haul on his shopping cart that he isn't in the same league, but Eddie gets angry anyway. He knows the other collector, as most collectors do when they cover the same area, and he doesn't like him. Not only does he owe Eddie money, but he is also coming too close to Eddie's turf at the wrong time.

"He's trying to get my building," Eddie says. "He knows that if he tries, I'll kill him."

Eddie doesn't really mean he'll kill the guy—at least I don't think he does—but it shows how seriously he takes his canning and how short-tempered he is after being out the whole night. By six A.M. he has filled ten huge bags that are strapped to his cart with numerous ropes, and the eight-foot structure is braced underneath by an array of broomsticks that allow the bags to be heaped as well as suspended.

"That's about a hundred bucks," he guesses, nodding at the bags.

Eddie, who is in his forties and short of build, supports not a drug habit from his collecting but a wife and two children. His routine of going from building to building is the exact opposite of Mr. Murphy's one-stop canning at SummerStage, which is also why he is less sanguine about it. Trudging the streets for hours and hours, night after night, is not something he wants to do for the rest of his life, but until he can find another job, he has no choice. In the meantime, he's getting older and the job is getting harder. As if it weren't bad enough that there are fewer cans around, seeing as it's summer and everyone is at the beach, they are being sought after by more canners than ever.

"There used to be two of us up here when I started seven years ago," he says about the area where he collects. During the months that his competitor went into rehab one year, it was only him. "But now there's a lot more."

After partly filling an eleventh bag, Eddie decides to call it a day and turn his cart onto Third Avenue to begin his trek of fifty-five blocks—almost three miles—to a redemption center in Harlem called the Bottle Place. He takes Third Avenue because it doesn't have as many hills as Park and Madison. By the time he reaches the Bottle Place, about thirty people are already inside the compact, fenced-off lot. Several other collectors stand on the sidewalk, patiently waiting to enter. They don't talk or acknowledge one another, both colleagues and competitors at the same time, and in between them are empty, unattended shopping carts that belong to the collectors inside. One cart is crisscrossed with a puzzle of broomsticks, the intricate framework that would support a dozen or more of Eddie's thirty-gallon bags, but with nothing on them now the construction resembles a gigantic game of Pickup Sticks.

Little about the Bottle Place reveals its identity as one of the most important redemption centers in the city. There are no big signs declaring, DEPOSITS FOR BOTTLES AND CANS HERE—5¢ EACH, but every canner knows the corner lot. Indeed, if you see someone in Manhattan pushing a cartload of empty cans, they are probably headed for Wecan, where Mr. Murphy goes, or the Bottle Place.

At first glance, the Bottle Place seems chaotic, with thousands of receptacles scattered everywhere. Three sides of the lot are bordered by small mountains of cans and bottles, and the people inside the congested space have to move very carefully to get from one corner to another. Yet everything happens with a kind of factory-line precision, and everyone is doing the same thing. Sorting. Collectors bend over their bags, pull out an item, and shove it into another bag or toss it onto growing mounds, count aloud, then write down their tallies on scrap pieces of paper or cardboard. The cans have to be divided into companies: Coca-Cola (and its subsidiaries), Pepsi (and its subsidiaries), the various beer companies, and Poland Spring mineral water. The sorters know the corporations as well as any Wall Street analyst: Coke owns Seagram's and Sprite, Pepsi has Mountain Dew, 7Up, Mugg, Schweppes. The bottles have to be further subdivided by size: one-liter, two-liter, thirty-ounce. Most bags take 240 cans or forty large bottles, and if a collector doesn't have enough to fill a bag, he is given a few small plastic crates.

The bespectacled man in charge of the Bottle Place is soft-spoken and, unlike the canners he deals with all the time, very friendly. He tells me that he pays out about two thousand dollars daily, which means he takes in about forty thousand items. At Wecan it can be as much as three thousand dollars. More than a hundred collectors turn up each day of the week, Sunday included, and their numbers keep growing. People who used to throw away their bottles and cans, or who even kept them for canners, like police stations and fire houses, now bring them in themselves to make some pocket money.

"Sometimes we have to chase the people away," the manager says.

Almost all the canners at the Bottle Place are regulars, and most of them are men. This particular weekday there are three women, one of whom—white, in her thirties, her suntanned skin leathery—finishes sorting her load and then watches the other canners, bleary-eyed, a cigarette hanging out the side of her mouth. A stooped old man carefully folds a plastic shopping bag, which couldn't have contained more than a few dollars' worth, then makes his way to a table, where he reports his total and receives his payout. The two people are so different that I can't help wonder what each one uses his or her takings for.

Because Mr. Murphy and Eddie consistently bring in so much to their respective redemption centers, the procedure is usually ironed out for them. Little waiting, few holdups. Mr. Murphy says he can be in and out of Wecan in three minutes. Not all canners get this treatment, but the deal is still a lot sweeter than elsewhere in the city. Most other redemption centers impose severe limitations, and some give only two dollars for twenty-four items, keeping the extra twenty cents for themselves. At a supermarket a few blocks away from the Bottle Place, a sign warns you there's a maximum: 240 ITEMS ONLY! Almost as offputting as the cap of twelve dollars is the process you have to go through to get it. At the store's seven machines, cans get sucked in by a rotator, while the bar code is read on anything plastic. Often the bar code isn't properly scanned or the can gets spat out, so they have to be put in over and over again, after which the machine might produce a receipt that hasn't been added up correctly. Despite all these frustrations, there is always a line at each machine.

Eddie tries to plan his morning routine in such a way that the Bottle Place is open by the time he gets there. Redemption centers work normal office hours, so if a canner finishes collecting at three A.M., he has to find somewhere safe to spend the next few hours. When Mr. Murphy needs to stay out for the night—he hasn't been homeless for four years, but it is usually inconvenient to take his load home with him—he heads to an office block in midtown that is known as a safe haven for canners. There are generally six or seven people there at night, and someone is always awake to guard the cans.

"I can go to sleep and know my stash will be there when I wake up," he says.

For anyone who doesn't want to wait until morning, there is an option: the two-for-one man, who gets his name from paying five cents for two cans, half the normal price. He usually has a vehicle, which he parks in a location convenient to canners, who regularly take advantage of his service even though they complain about him exploiting their predicament. The brilliance of this hustle—doubling your money overnight by doing practically nothing—is not lost on Mr. Murphy. He has seriously considered becoming a two-for-one man himself.

"You don't have to go around killing yourself. All you have to do is count the cans, bag them, and transport them. It's not robbery. I'm not putting a gun to your head, telling you to do it. You are coming willingly. It's a good business."

Leaving the Bottle Place, I see the last two canners of the morning standing on the sidewalk, one with a shopping cart and the other with a laundry cart. They remind me, and not for the first time, of a photograph taken more than a hundred years ago by Alice Austen. In it two ragpickers on a New York street are taking a rest alongside their two-wheeled wooden carts, both of which are piled high with overstuffed bags.

The bags and their contents today might be different—plastic instead of burlap, cans instead of rags—but their owners still have to push their carts and they still go after something nobody else wants. If there has been a change over the last century, it is that ragpickers back then were immigrants, often Italians, who used scrap collecting as a way to get ahead in their new country. The only canner I meet who fits that profile today, though, is Manuel, who comes from Ecuador.

Canning wasn't Manuel's first job in this country. He took the route of many Hispanic immigrants, doing odd jobs for a gardening service on Long Island and working shifts in a clothing factory. The most he has made from canning in a day is one hundred dollars, which doesn't compare to Eddie or Mr. Murphy, but it's not bad for someone who crossed the border into Texas with barely enough money to make a call on a pay phone.

"In the beginning it was terrible, and I didn't know where to find the cans," he says in Spanish. His English is still limited to the world of what he collects: *one-liter, two-liter, thirty ounce, Coca-Cola, Snapple.* "I made maybe four dollars a day. I felt like crying."

Manuel doesn't look or dress like most canners, whether it's Baldy, who goes shirtless, or the Pimp, who gets his name from his gaudy outfits. Manuel wears a jacket and dark trousers, his shirt is shiny with a pattern down the side, the collar stiffly starched, and his hair is combed across his forehead, two specks of dandruff caught at the sharp oiled edges. A copy of *Reader's Digest Selecciones* sticks out of his jacket pocket. He could be a peasant in the South American countryside walking to Sunday mass rather than a canner on his way to the Bottle Place. Nor is he evasive and antisocial like most canners, but always smiling and ready to talk.

"It pays to be nice," Manuel says, echoing Mr. Murphy's dictum about behavior being premeditated and potentially lucrative. "It pays to say, 'I'm sorry, lady,' if you bump into someone by accident. Then they help you out. People remember you and keep things for you."

Not that friendliness and a readiness to talk to strangers always work. People come up to him and berate him for not having a job when he is young and healthy. Others offer him money, but he tells them he isn't looking for handouts.

"But I take it anyway," he says, then winks at me.

Manuel cans in East Harlem, where he also lives. He wakes at five every morning of the week, Saturday and Sunday included, makes himself breakfast, and is out on the road by six-fifteen A.M. He is too new to have his own buildings, at least not any big ones, but there are a few smaller places that keep cans for him. He has also learned which buildings to avoid, because they belong to other canners or the maintenance people don't tolerate loiterers. At midday he goes home for two hours to eat, listen to music, sleep, read, and write in his diary. On one side of the page he lists his total expenses for the day. *January 4, $4, February 2, $3.* On the other side he lists the money he has made from cans and bottles. *January 14, $29. March 4, $35. April 15, $50.* By early afternoon, he is ready for the second half of his working day, when he goes to cash in his cans, after which, from six o'clock until eight, he collects again.

When Manuel left his hometown of Guayacapa at the beginning of 2000, he also left behind his wife and four children, as well as his job as a bookkeeper. He wanted to make enough money in the United States—about ten or twelve thousand dollars, he estimates—so that he could return to Ecuador and open his own business. But only a few years later, his goals have changed, and you can't help thinking that soda cans, and the ease with which they're found, have had something to do with it.

"Now I'll try make a million," he says, then laughs, although it sounds like he thinks it's quite possible.

Manuel wasn't the first person in his family to immigrate to America. His two elder brothers came a dozen years before him, both paying to stow away in the banana container of a boat that sailed from Machala, in southern Ecuador, to Los Angeles. They were given food, water, and a bag to defecate in.

"They were just like the bananas," Manuel matter-of-factly says.

His own trip was just as uncomfortable but not nearly as quick or direct. He was one of 120 people who were squeezed onto a fishing boat that sailed north from the port of Guayaquil. They got caught by a coastal patrol off Guatemala and were left floating at sea for eight days, the boat's engine damaged, before being taken to Tegucigalpa and then sent home.

A week after arriving back in Ecuador, an undeterred Manuel was on another boat, this one with about ninety aboard. When they reached Guatemala, they were split into smaller groups and were then led to the interior, where they waited outside Quezaltenango for fifteen days. They had eaten almost nothing on the boat and were hungry and malnourished.

"The *federales* caught me one day, but I acted as if I was Guatemalan and they let me go. They menaced other people, mistreated them. They hit them on the legs."

From Quezaltenango they crossed into the volatile Mexican region of Chiapas. Manuel was in a group of eight, and they walked mostly at night and slept in fields during the day. To cross the long lakes east of the Sierra Madre mountains they lay flat on manmade rafts and drifted along the water.

"It was dangerous in Chiapas, yes. But that's because of things like this, the trafficking of people."

After heading for Veracruz on the Gulf of Mexico, they proceeded up the coast to the border town of Matamoros. On April 1, more than a month after sailing from Ecuador, Manuel and his group crossed the Rio Grande into the United States. They were almost immediately detected by a border patrol, and everyone fled in different directions. Some of them got caught, but Manuel managed to hide. Now on his own, he followed a railroad track for a day before meeting two Mexicans with whom he teamed up. The Mexicans knew some people outside San Antonio, and when he got there Manuel phoned his brothers in Los Angeles. They wired him money, and after giving twenty dollars to each of the Mexicans, he bought a ticket on what he calls "the bus of the dogs," Greyhound. Eleven days after crossing the border, and forty-five days after leaving Ecuador, he reached New York.

"I am still illegal," he says, "but I'm not doing anything illegal."

He no longer talks to his brothers, because they don't approve of his collecting.

"They think I'm crazy. They accuse me of dedicating myself to picking up cans and bottles. I tell them that if I was working in a sweatshop or a restaurant, I would have no time for anything. I do this because I like it and I am free."

The freedom Manuel mentions is different from the kind many immigrants once came to America for, and possibly still do, not political or social but personal, a freedom to be outdoors, away from an office, working according to their own schedule and rules. Canning, of course, has its own limitations, as does every kind of collecting I come across. In spite of this, being free is something that every collector prizes almost as much as the mongo itself.

chapter 3

the treasure hunter

Long before nightfall, when most canners go out, Dave gathers his spade, rubber gloves, and hard hat, and then heads off in search of mongo. Like the canners, though, Dave sticks to a particular location, one where he's been very lucky in the past and he's sure to find stuff again.

For several years before I met Dave, his favorite location had been a small section of land on the bank of the Hudson River. Every day he would leave the diner where he works and walk four blocks west to the river. While most people were going to the Hudson to jog, walk their dogs, watch the boats sail by, or just hang out, Dave had something else in mind altogether. Namely, dirt.

The city was widening the West Side Highway, which runs along the river, and at regular intervals lay piles of gravel and sand. To the tens of thousands of motorists who passed the heaps daily, they were nothing extraordinary, a temporary nuisance they had to circumnavigate. To Dave they contained something much more valuable. Since the dirt had probably come from under the West Side Highway, it stood a good chance of being landfill.

It has been estimated that as much as a third of Lower Manhattan is landfill. When the first settlers sailed into New York Bay, there were shores, marshes, inlets, and streams that have disappeared over the centuries. Hills were flattened to fill cavities, and tons of earth and garbage were thrown into the water between piers to extend the land. Eventually those piers too were swallowed by new land.

Battery Park is landfill, and so is South Street, Front Street, and much of Water Street. Parts of Greenwich Village around Gansevoort Street are landfill. Rikers Island grew to almost twice its size with the addition of landfill and garbage. And the West Side Highway is built on landfill.

To determine whether land is or isn't landfill, many architects and contractors use the *Sanitary and Topographical Map of the City and Island of New York*. Drawn up more than a century ago by George Waring's former boss, Egbert Vielé, who classified terrain as Marsh, Made land, or Meadow, it remains one of the most authoritative documents available.

With the map dating back to 1865, and the first landfill originating two centuries before that, it's anybody's guess what was discarded in the newly created areas. The contents of landfill were not well documented, and although historians have noted that they were dumping grounds for garbage, animal carcasses, and river mud, they could contain lots more. And that's exactly what keeps Dave digging.

Dave had his first contact with landfill in the mid-1980s. A friend of his, Scott, was snooping around after hours at a construction site in Battery Park, all of which is landfill. After the bulldozers and Caterpillars had left for the day, Scott and his digging partner, Zach, would arrive to sift through what had been uncovered. They had already found antique bottles and pieces of pottery, as well as old brass medals and buttons from the Revolutionary War.

Late one night they were forty feet down when Scott's metal

detector went berserk. As he dug up the area, which was about nine feet in length, he uncovered the front, middle, and then the back of a cannon that had a ball handle as big as a cantaloupe. He didn't have the time or the equipment to lift a four-thousand-pound weapon four stories to the street, so he left it.

"It's probably sitting in some contractor's garden today," he says twenty years later.

If Scott has any regrets about the cannon, an even bigger trophy awaited him and Zach. When the construction company's excavation came to an end, they hitched a lift with one of the dump trucks to the site on Staten Island where the landfill was being off-loaded. There they walked along a pathway that led through tons and tons of landfill, the mud and garbage that had been used centuries earlier to fill in Manhattan's shoreline.

On top of one of the piles, both of them spied something at the same moment and then ran for it. Zach got there first and grabbed the object. It looked like a cowboy hat, but as they knocked off the black mud they noticed that the brim could be folded in three places. They both immediately knew what it was: a tricorn hat from the Revolutionary War. Several years later, Zach took it to *Antiques Roadshow*, where it was valued at nine thousand dollars.

After hearing about the tricorn hat, there was no doubt in Dave's mind that centuries-old garbage that was once used to fill up the depressions in the city's topography could be the gold of today. And much like a precious metal, it lies in veins. In some parts of the city, that "gold" might be deep down, forty feet or more, but elsewhere, in the southernmost parts where the settlers first arrived, something of value might be hidden only a few inches below street level.

Dave went out sporadically at first, and then, as he grew more successful, practically every night. He started looking for new sites. At Pier 57, where the city was digging to lay a new sewer, he found hundreds of bottles. At another site he found dozens of cannonballs.

Soon his landfill maps were never far from him—he compares old and new maps to see where land is that wasn't there before—and he had a sixth sense for landfill. "Anywhere near the water is good," he once told me, talking about suitable places to search, "and then you just look at the dirt. If there's shards, it's a good sign." He developed a knack for spotting piles of excavated landfill on the side of the road, even if he was driving past at a substantial speed, and he could date the landfill to within a few decades by quickly perusing its contents. If there was landfill being dug up in Manhattan, chances were good that Dave would be snooping around the neighborhood.

The West Side Highway, however, introduced him to a totally new kind of landfill. Wandering there one evening, sifting at random through gravel, one pile in particular caught his attention. He didn't know it at the time, but not only did the gravel come from under the city but it came from the pipes under the city. It wasn't dirt but leftover sludge, or sediment.

Dave still glows when he recalls that night.

"I was looking for bottles and suddenly I saw this gold chain sticking out of a pile. Gold! There it was, just waiting to be found." It wasn't a tricorn hat from the Revolutionary War, but it came pretty close. "I saw a construction guy nearby and I said, 'Hey, where does this pile come from?' and he said, 'The sewers.'"

Dave had chanced upon a whole new kind of mongo. Up

till then he had been happy to find old buttons, torpedo bottles, and seventeenth-century bricks, items he knew had some kind of value, although it was often difficult to ascertain exactly what that was. How much, for instance, does one charge for a yellow brick brought from Holland four centuries ago?

But jewelry was another thing altogether. It was easier to classify and to put a price on. And if there was a gold chain in this sediment, he wondered, could old rings and bracelets be far behind? Maybe he would even find a diamond or two.

Long before Dave got to landfill, long before he reached the West Side Highway, he owned a metal detector. As a child he loved stories about pirates and buried treasure, and a metal detector seemed like a good modern-day substitute for a treasure map. He bought his first metal-detecting kit at RadioShack, but he could never get it to work. By the time he reached college, in Oklahoma, he was metal detecting regularly, and when he moved to New York after graduation he got serious about it.

He crisscrossed every public garden, from Battery Park to Tompkins Square Park to Central Park. When the city started renovating Madison Square Park, created in 1847 and one of the oldest parks in the city, Dave got into the cordoned-off area by bribing the security guard with beers. It paid off, and he found three-cent silver coins and two-cent coppers from the 1850s and 1860s, as well as tiny half dimes dating as far back as 1794.

When the city demanded a license from people who wanted to enter the parks to do metal detecting—or what is sometimes called coin shooting—Dave got a license. But regulations finally became so tight that the pastime lost much of its allure. The actual luster of what he found was fading fast too.

"Every park has been picked so clean that you don't come up with much anymore," Dave says.

The only park likely to still contain anything is Central Park, which was where Dave found one of his best coins ever, a gold five-dollar Indian from 1912, right behind the Metropolitan Museum of Art. But Central Park was declared off-limits in 1985.

"Now that's their [the city's] baby," he tells me.

Dave is peeved that the authorities have closed off New York's most famous and potentially lucrative park, because he believes they did it not so much to keep people like him out but to give park officials the freedom to metal-detect there by themselves.

If collectors like Dave have one obvious trait, it's resilience. When one door closes, they search for another. They look for new items, different areas, and they change their focus. The can collectors adapt whenever the city alters its recycling policy. Sarah lowered her expectations when she returned to the city in the 1980s, looking uptown instead of downtown. Dave, meanwhile, took his metal detector to other pieces of open ground. He went to beaches in particular, even though a long stretch of sand is a lot tougher to crack than a park.

"You've got to know what you're doing—and when to do it. The best time for the beach is after a big storm, when the old sand's washed away and a fresh layer's been uncovered."

It was on a beach not far from where Dave lives, Brighton Beach, that his favorite story about a collector took place. Or was it an urban legend? After a heavy storm, a metal detector went out and found twenty pieces of gold in the sand, all stuck together in one big clump.

"Maybe it wasn't twenty pieces," Dave says on reflection. "Maybe the whole story got blown out of proportion. It could have been just two or three coins."

The sober afterthought is typical of Dave. Whenever he talks about a discovery, whether it's his own or someone else's, he allows himself to get carried away for only the briefest moment. He's not starry-eyed about collecting, and he never forgets that even though there are plenty of highs, like finding the gold chain on the West Side Highway or the five-dollar Indian, there are just as many lows, like going for months without finding anything. But he implicitly believes that, big or small, there is a pot of gold at the end of the rainbow, and the rainbow's end could be as near as Brighton Beach.

Dave still uses his metal detector on occasion. In the trunk of his car is a Garrett GTA 1000 that he takes out when he's at a loose end, which means there isn't better stuff to look for elsewhere. The Garrett is like the faithful mistress he goes back to when the others fail him: She's reliable, predictable, but not particularly exciting. In all his time using the Garrett —he is on his fourth model now—he never came across a silver dollar or a gold ring. He would find both on the West Side Highway. And more, a lot more.

After the night when Dave spotted the gold chain in the pile of sediment, he kept returning to the location. Whenever he saw a dump truck arriving with a new load, he sought out the driver, talked to him, joked with him. As he always does on a new site, Dave made sure to get permission to dig.

There was no problem getting access to the site—as far as the driver was concerned, it was just sludge and muck—and

Dave's manner is so slow and disarming that no one would suspect that he was asking if he could dig for gold there.

"The driver said, 'Sure, go through it, I don't care.'"

The company hauling the sediment was one of several contracted by the city to clean the sewers of Manhattan. By 1890, New York had more than four hundred miles of sewers, most of them made of brick and wide enough for a man to walk in upright. By 1902, there were fourteen hundred miles. Some of the sewers hadn't been cleaned for a long time, if ever, so when the huge hoses were finally brought in to spray them down, they loosened plenty of things that were in their path.

"It's stuff that had been stuck there for, what, maybe a hundred years," says Dave.

The grime, grit, sand, construction debris, even dislodged bricks were sucked up, and once everything had been hauled to the West Side Highway, it was off-loaded onto piles and into Dumpsters. (Much later it would be mixed with other gravel and sand to create more landfill.)

At that point Dave's work commenced. In the back of his car, next to the Garrett, are a rake, a spade for serious digging, sticks for poking the earth when a more gentle approach is required, a sieve, and various gloves. Rake in one hand, a hand sifter in the other, he would climb into a Dumpster.

"The sifter's how you get the little things, pieces of chain, lockets, stones. You can never be too careful. Sometimes you get rings without stones. Sometimes stones without rings."

One of the stones he found by sifting through a sediment-filled Dumpster was a $1\frac{3}{4}$-carat diamond.

Whenever Dave has to use his hands to burrow into the sediment, he wears at least three layers of protection: two pairs of rubber gloves and one pair of gardening gloves. The sediment is usually still moist, and even though it's not dangerous to handle, an infection could get into a cut on his hand.

"It's not as bad as some people think. When I explain to them where my stuff comes from, some of them are totally disgusted. They go, 'Eee-ew, the sewers! That's gross! I can't touch that, it's been in doo-dee.'"

If people who find out the origin of Dave's jewelry are astonished, it's more by the fact that his gold and diamonds were originally covered in feces than that they come from the sewers of New York. Dave's recourse is simple: He just doesn't tell people where his mongo comes from.

In truth, the unburied bijouterie is hardly ever very dirty, and all Dave has to do is give each bauble a quick rub with a jewelry rag.

"Nothing I find really smells that terrible," he adds, taking obvious delight in describing the more vulgar aspects of his pastime. "Truth is, most of the bad stuff has been washed away by water and urine. So what comes out is hardly even sludge. Remember, sludge is fecal matter. This stuff is more like sediment. It depends on where it comes from, but sediment is usually looser and not so oily."

It didn't take Dave long to learn how to read the caliber of sediment: poor, mediocre, or the mother lode. The truck drivers didn't know from one day to the next where they would be sent to clean up. When they found out, they would tell Dave, but often he had to guess the origin of what they off-loaded. If he knew, then he also knew what to expect—for the contents of a pipe below, say, the tenement houses of the Bowery differ vastly from whatever lies under the palatial apartments of Sutton Place.

"In the poorer neighborhoods, people couldn't afford gold or quality jewelry, so you'll find cheap rings, dime-store stuff. None of it migrates very far from where it falls. It just sits in the main sewer line until they clean it, even if that's a century later."

Little Italy is where Dave had his first major windfall—twenty-two gold rings in ninety minutes—all of it what he calls "quality stuff." He shows me one of the rings when we meet one day at the diner where he is the accountant. The ring, which is studded with a ruby, a sapphire, and two diamonds, also happens to be the last of the twenty-two he has left. All the others he sold or gave away. His sister got the best, a platinum maternity band with thirty diamonds running around its circumference. Only after he'd given it to her did he find out that it was worth fifteen hundred dollars.

"If only I'd known that at the time," he says, then laughs.

I can't tell whether Dave really means that he would never have given the ring away if he'd known its value. Value, in any case, is one of the first things that he brings up, not historical but monetary. In contrast to Nelson, he always mentions what price he got for an object, what he could have gotten, or what he might get. In his apartment there are price guides for old toys, bottles, Americana, anything that he might find in his digs. A well-thumbed copy of *Kovels' Antiques & Collectibles Price List* is always close at hand. He mentions what an object is worth so frequently, in fact, you might think that is all he's interested in, and that the specter of treasure is the only thing that lures him out into the filth.

On his desk at the diner he has laid out a tumulus of trinkets for me to look through. They look like hundreds of curtain rings but, on closer inspection, turn out to be spoons, crosses, rings, faceless cameos, and twisted stickpins and bracelets. As he sits behind them, he resembles a modern-day Shylock, an impression that is only heightened by his physical appearance, for he is wearing four silver rings, has a scrappy week-old beard and a little ponytail, and his fingernails are chewed halfway down to the base. One of the first things he tells me is how much money he has made from his subterranean discoveries in the last four years: twenty thousand dollars.

The more I get to know Dave, however, the more I see that selling what he digs up, and then getting as much as he can for it, isn't nearly as important as I first believed. One day, for instance, he finds a medallion inscribed with the words "Gratefully yours, Johnny Ray," a memento probably given out by the hundreds at the height of the singer's career. When Dave reads in the newspaper about a Johnny Ray revival at a jazz club downtown, he heads there with the keepsake, fully intending to find a buyer. But he is so moved by the evening and by the singer's fans that he gives one of them the medallion as a present.

"He was so excited," Dave says.

At least three quarters of all the objects Dave has uncovered remain unsold and are packed away in his apartment. Next to the front door is a large bucket of old cutlery that is so full it's impossible to move. Seven years ago, his friend Scott asked him to gather some silver that he wanted to use in his artwork. Even though Scott gave up that project a few months later, Dave hasn't stopped collecting knives, forks, and spoons.

His passionate desire to collect doesn't always do the other passionate side of him any good. His second wife, though she joined him collecting when they first met, eventually left him because of it.

"It was the collecting and other things," he adds in his defense.

Two walls of Dave's apartment are covered in bottles, and there is a small pile of broken clay pipes in a showcase. Several jars of marbles stand in one corner, ranging from large colorful clay ones to the better-known glass Swirls. Dave has about six thousand marbles, which he says probably ended up in the sewers when kids were playing with them in the streets and shot them into the storm drains. Some of them are old enough to have even been swept there by members of the old street-sweeping department of the nineteenth century.

Marbles are about the only thing that Dave doesn't read up on. He might have thousands, but they bore him. Most other objects he looks up in the series of books that he has positioned close to his easy chair. Occasionally, when he can't find a history for them, he makes one up, the same way Sarah does, although his speculation is probably closer to the truth. He doesn't expect you to take him seriously, but it helps him give some context and meaning to an artifact that might otherwise remain anonymous. Story-making also helps pass away the long hours when you're out looking in the sediment.

Sometimes it even feels like he's doing a bit of detective work. Take, for instance, his explanation about a certain batch of false teeth. Dave occasionally finds false teeth, and, as a kind of ghoulish reminder, keeps a pair lying on the top of a huge bowl of sewer curios in his living room. In a single load of sediment that came from underneath the East Village, he once found a dozen sets of teeth all at once.

To demystify this bizarre bonanza, he tells you to picture

a guy who regularly came home drunk, got sick during the night, vomited into the toilet, and lost his dentures in the process. Waking up toothless the following day, he would go out and get a new pair, only to lose them in exactly the same way the next time he went drinking.

For most of the things he finds, Dave has a more simple explanation for how they ended up in the sewer. They accidentally got dropped into the toilet, went down the sink and bathtub drains when the openings were bigger, or got swept into the storm drains. These items include metal buttons, old subway tokens, World War II dog tags, glass beads, a silver keyhole, hypodermic needles, a metal chauffeur's license from the 1920s, and bullets, both used and live.

When Dave has a stand at a flea market, which he often does, he seldom expounds on all the things he's learned or relates the stories he's invented. He doesn't care for small talk. That could be one of the reasons why he sells only one out of every four objects and why he rarely gets its true value. One antique sapphire ring he sold for only twenty-five dollars.

Another reason is it's not easy to marry a specific item with the right buyer. Luckily for Dave, he has several regular clients. A colleague at the diner bought four gold rings. A New York author of books about Revolutionary War memorabilia used to buy his white gold. Other collectors come to him for old keys; certain kinds of marbles, especially Benningtons and Swirls; old metal toys that once came in cereal boxes; store tokens; silver dollars and half dimes, which come out of the sewer washed as thin as paper. One collector bought all his religious memorabilia, about a hundred crosses and sacred medals; and any loose gold Dave has—a mangled brooch here, a single earring there—he sells in bulk to a dealer on Forty-seventh Street.

Occasionally there are takers for the unusual and the bizarre, such as an old postal badge ("This guy I know just had to have it, and he gave me a hundred bucks for it"), a turn-of-the-century police whistle (someone wanted it, but Dave donated it to the Police Museum), and a set of false teeth embedded with gold.

In early 2000, Dave's luck came to an end as abruptly as the construction work on the West Side Highway. The contractors started dumping the sediment from New York's sewers at another site outside the city, and even though Dave tried to find out where that was, he failed.

He resorted to his old ways. He took out his trusty mistress, the Garrett, and went metal detecting. He regularly checked out construction sites to see if there was any landfill, and he sized up every Dumpster he passed, just to make sure its contents weren't sediment. Every Saturday and Sunday he got into his car and drove, with no particular destination in mind, going farther afield, into neighboring states, constantly keeping his eyes peeled for any evidence of landfill. He rode along the cobbled roads of Peck Slip and Catherine Slip, near South Street Seaport, mainly in search of roadwork; a bulldozer could, without much effort, uncover landfill just a few inches down. But he came across very little.

Even when Dave wasn't out looking for sludge, it was never far from his mind. If he wasn't dreaming of finding a new dump site, then he was fantasizing about the day when the sewer cleaners might drain those parts of the city where he was certain he would find gold. Possibility number one was under Forty-seventh Street, where an acquaintance of his was coming out of a jewelry store with his wife when her forty-

thousand-dollar ring fell into the sewer. ("It's just sitting in a
pipe down there.") Possibility number 2 was under London
Terrace, a gargantuan apartment complex built in the early
1930s in Chelsea. ("Gangsters were supposed to have lived
there. All their girlfriends had jewelry, and I bet some of it
went down the drain.")

Whenever Dave returned from his exploratory outings, he
was carrying a few twenty-dollar antique bottles he'd picked
out of a dump here or fifty dollars' worth of gold he had
found in a Dumpster there. But when you are used to
unearthing fifteen-hundred-dollar maternity bands and a score
of gold rings all at the same time, those finds seemed piffling.

Every time I talked to Dave on the phone, he sounded list-
less, as if the years on the West Side Highway were golden,
in more ways than one, and he didn't expect to be reliving
them anytime soon.

"It's very boring when you find nothing," he said and sighed.

Then, exactly a year after the West Side Highway dried up,
Dave found not one site but two, and within weeks of each
other. The first was a yard in Brooklyn where sediment was
being deposited. It wasn't nearly as accessible as the West Side
Highway, and to get into it Dave had to scale a fence topped
with razor wire. As a result, he had added to his digging acces-
sories a padded blanket, which he tossed across the fence to
protect himself. Fence scaling late at night sounded like the
kind of thing that could land Dave in jail, but he assured me
that it was entirely legal.

Even though his initial discoveries didn't amount to much,
he seemed rejuvenated, as happy as a pig in mud. One day
when I visited him at the diner, he pulled out a small plastic
bag containing what he had found the previous night. It was

all gold, but none of it exceptional: a cross, a heart-shaped locket, a brooch with the stone missing, and an old tooth casing.

"You can tell these people didn't have money. The cross is nice. You'll get fifty bucks for all of it, unless you sell it separately."

Looking at the small brooches and bits of chain, I couldn't imagine how he managed to sift them from piles of sediment in the dark of night or, for that matter, why he would bother.

"One of the construction guys told me he found a ring worth five thousand," Dave said, the glint back in his eye. "He wasn't looking for stuff, he just saw it."

But before he could find anything valuable at the Brooklyn yard, the contractors brought in a load of sediment that was so greasy that not even Dave, wearing his protective uniform of boots and triple gloves, was prepared to tackle it.

In the following weeks, as he waited for new sediment to be dumped over the greasy load, Dave came across a second site while driving around New Jersey. The contents of the site were almost the exact opposite of landfill, what you might call "riverfill." A piece of land was being covered with mud extracted from the bottom of the Hudson River.

One Sunday, Dave takes me to the mud. First he drives past Peck Slip and Catherine Slip, just to make sure that, even though it's the weekend, there's no roadwork going on. Then he makes a quick stop at a Dumpster, where it takes him a few seconds to determine that it contains only barren gravel.

After the Holland Tunnel we turn onto a highway outside Jersey City, but Dave suddenly slows down. He has spotted something. He takes a series of turnoffs that lead us back to the road we were on, and after a few more turns he parks the car in a small lot between several empty vehicles and a broken-down trailer. To the side of the trailer I see what caught Dave's attention, even though he was driving by at fifty miles per hour: two mounds of earth, each one only about three feet high.

"Landfill," he says.

His eye falls on a piece of plate sticking out of one of the mounds. He tugs at it, and a small triangle comes loose. He inspects the name on the fragment: *British & North American Steamship Royal Mail Steam Packing*.

"Could be from anywhere. Looks like eighteen nineties. Maybe eighteen sixties."

There're bits of shell in the dirt too, as well as segments of bottle, but Dave has already drawn his conclusion.

"Nothing here."

Before leaving he picks up a few pink limbs from a modern doll that lie scattered about. They are for Scott's artwork, he says. The trunk of Dave's car contains other things for Scott—fragments of pottery, cracked bottlenecks, porcelain shards. Alongside them are Dave's tools, his Garrett, a hard hat that he uses when he needs to disguise himself as a construction worker, several of the yellow bricks from Dutch settler days, and numerous old soda bottles coated in rich dark mud.

"My house already has so much crap in it," he explains unnecessarily.

In one corner of the trunk are about a dozen more bottles, green Coca-Colas, some dating back to the 1920s, although none of them are particularly valuable. Dave puts them out on his stand at the flea market.

"Japanese tourists will pay twenty dollars for those. It's a piece of America and it's a pretty green color."

Even though Dave has found diamonds and gold worth thousands of dollars, he won't reject an item that might fetch only a couple of bucks.

"I'm into all realms," he says. "I just like getting dirty."

After we leave the twin mounds of landfill, Dave gets lost on the highway. It's a good omen, and he hopes that the river-fill will be equally difficult for anyone else to find too. He would prefer to keep the potentially lucrative site a secret from other collectors for as long as possible.

"One guy I wanted to sell this jar to [that came from the riverfill] asked me where I got it, so I said Pennsylvania. To put him off the track, you see. Otherwise he would have been here in a second. It gets people crazy. As soon as I show things to them, there's problems. They want to know where it came from. I'm not finding enough that I want a zoo down here."

Dave talks about the river mud as "part two." He doesn't need to explain that part one was the West Side Highway. The way he sees it, he is being given a second chance. The geography of the site is different from what he's used to—the sediment is from the bottom of the river versus from the bottom of the city, the artifacts are bottles and porcelain versus jewelry, false teeth, and bullets, and they are spread over several acres of mud versus in a Dumpster—but the returns could be just as good. The jar Dave dug up on an earlier visit was an intact, blue-rimmed clay jar dating to the mid-nineteenth century, and the same day he found an 1848 eight-sided cobalt blue W. P. Knickerbocker soda bottle. He sold the jar for $350 and the bottle for $275.

"Six hundred and a quarter," he says, smiling. "Good for a day's work."

As is his custom, Dave conjures a history for the mud,

guessing from the bits of porcelain and glass that the antiq-
uities might date back as much as three centuries.

"They were probably in a ship that was blown up during
a battle."

Before we reach the site, which is on New York Bay, we
drive through a suburb of row houses, where kids hang out
on the streets between broken-down cars, and then pass a
cemetery and go under a narrow railway track. It's hard to
imagine how Dave stumbled onto the river mud during a
casual Sunday drive, but then it's safe to assume that Dave's
casual Sunday drive is like no one else's.

Somewhere on a nondescript piece of flat road between an
army reserve station and a new town house development, we
turn onto a dirt track and then come to an abrupt halt. A huge
log bars the way, clearly placed there to keep trespassers like
us out. We roll it to one side, and once Dave has driven through
I push it back into place. Right before he drives in, Dave spots
a lone police car on the main road, so he waits until it has left
the area. His surreptitious actions suggest that we are here ille-
gally, but once again he assures me that he has gotten the green
light to dig. For the first time, I'm not too sure he has.

"The guy who drives the Caterpillar said it was okay," he
adds. "I'm the only one allowed in here."

On the far side of a small rise is our destination, two flat-
topped hills of mud, and Dave parks on the track running in
between them. As we climb one of the hills, he explains that
the first load of river mud was deposited six weeks earlier, on
top of which more mud has been added several times already.
Eventually, the owner will flatten the terrain to build a golf
course. Until then, or until someone else finds out about the
site or Dave is denied access, he has it all to himself.

"It's like your own little world here," he says.

Even before we start crisscrossing the hills, Dave is pretty confident that we won't find anything. It's too soon after his last visit, and there hasn't been a good downpour since then to uncover the next layer of bottles and plates. He's so convinced that he leaves his gloves and spade in the car, taking only a stick to poke the hard ground with. As we make our way across the hills, which rise as much as fifteen feet in places, Dave imagines the treasure that we are walking over.

"When I first got here, I found twenty-five bottles sticking out—torpedoes, Bristol Creams, iron-pontilled sodas, nail bottles—so you've got to know how much more is hidden underneath."

The only problem is getting to it. With each day that the sun has baked the earth, the ground has formed a harder crust, and there's little chance of getting anything out unless it's close to the surface. We could use the Garrett, but metal detectors don't work well in clay. As we head off in different directions, Dave instructs me to watch out for any glint in the dry fissures that have started to appear.

"Look for shells and mica stone. That means you're near the bottom [of the river mud]. When you see broken pottery, you know you're at an active layer where there's bottles."

The only bottles I see are the broken and uninteresting ones Dave has already found on his previous visits, now lying tossed to the sides of the dump. Faced with such a huge terrain to inspect and so little that's sticking out—it feels as pointless as looking for a coin on an acre of grass—I quickly lose interest.

From where I am standing I can see a neat green field, where a Little League baseball game is about to start and someone is playing "The Star-Spangled Banner" on a bugle, a scene that heightens the bizarreness of what we are doing. In the distance vehicles speed along a highway, and I wonder what motorists might be thinking when they see two people walking aimlessly around a dump site where they shouldn't be. *Those people are up to no good.* Later in the day, when we pull up at another dump down a dead-end road, Dave himself will put my thoughts into words. "This is the kind of place you'd expect to find a body." For that reason alone he doesn't stick around the dead end for long, but his mention of a crime highlights the fact that there is always about the act of mongo collecting something illicit and, as a result, exhilarating.

While I wander aimlessly around the riverfill, Dave continues searching with purpose. He knows what to look for, and he knows how to look for it, whether it's in the confines of a Dumpster or spread over a vast expanse of river mud.

"I have good eyes," he tells me. "I can spot things."

It is the collector's gift, to pick out an item on the sidewalk, in the Dumpster, in a pile of landfill, the way a real collector would find something of value in an antiques store. And Dave does just that. In no time, he has found numerous articles, pieces of porcelain mostly, and several bottles. One of them, medium-sized and not particularly remarkable looking, has the word *Merriam's* written across its front.

As Dave was pulling the Merriam's out of the mud, he noticed a hairline crack in the neck. It expanded bit by bit, until the bottle finally broke. From his experience, Dave can tell that the crack probably developed only when it was dumped here a few days earlier. Sadly, a bottle that had survived under tons of mud for a century or more broke at the last minute.

How sad this actually is, however, Dave will discover only later on. When he gets home he tries to research the Merriam's, but he can't find any information about it. He asks his collector friends, but no one seems to have heard of it. After several days he comes across a single mention of a Merriam's—and the news is not good, at least not for Dave. When a Merriam's last came up for auction, it sold for more than five thousand dollars. Repaired, this one might sell for a few hundred.

Dave decides after that to give the river mud a break for a while, or at least until contractors add a new layer of mud. He returns to his second site, the sediment dump in Brooklyn, where by now the greasy load that drove him away has been covered with fresh muck. For two weeks Dave finds nothing special, just the usual pieces of gold, but one night he calls to tell me about an exciting development. He thinks he has found something that could be very valuable. It's a brass ring that bears the inscription SUPERMAN RING OF AMERICA. Dating back to 1939, it is the kind of curio that would've been bought from Action Comics for a nickel.

"The ring used to be painted," he says, adding an explanation I have come to expect from him, "but this one lost all its paint from years and years in the sewers."

Dave buffs up the Superman ring and puts it up for sale on an Internet site called Hake's Americana & Collectibles. The starting bid is five hundred dollars. Although some offers come in over the following weeks, and the price jumps a few hundred dollars at a time, nothing spectacular happens. Then, in the final days of the auction, two people start bidding against each other.

Dave can hardly contain himself when he calls me at the end of the month to tell me the news. Even before he says what he got for the ring, I can tell that he has reached the pot of gold at the end of this particular rainbow. The final bid was $9,387.

chapter 4

the anarchists

The chocolate-covered strawberries probably sell for five dollars each, but it sounds like they're worth a lot more. They are still cold, as if they had come straight from the fridge, and you'd never guess they were lying in a bag on the sidewalk for at least an hour on a hot summer's night. Channing passes one of the chocolates to Miles. Flo is already eating hers.

"Yay," says Flo, like a schoolgirl on a field trip, then takes another bite.

Flo was the first one to suspect that there might be something in the bag, because she saw that it was still tied up with a piece of string. "The red string means that no one else has been here yet." On opening the bag, Channing had to dig for only a few seconds before finding a cake box covered in wet coffee granules. Inside were the three chocolates, one for each of them.

Even though Miles isn't part of Flo and Channing's group, they always offer him a portion of whatever they find. Miles accepts the chocolate without hesitating, then gulps it down.

"That's the best thing I've ever tasted," he says, wiping his face with a soiled hand.

Channing says he's seen and tasted better. In Austin, Texas, where he spent the past few winters, he came across a five-gallon drum of solid chocolate—not once, but several times.

You can hear from his tone of voice that certain items rate much higher than everything else.

"We've also found whole crates of soy milk and a load of maple syrup and waffle mix. Whole crates! We fed a crew of fifty people out of the Dumpsters. I've found bikes, even library Dumpsters." After a brief pause Channing concludes, "Austin is the best place in the world for Dumpster diving."

The chocolate-covered strawberries come from a black bag, but no ordinary black bag, seeing it's situated outside Delice, one of the best cake shops in New York. That means its contents are pretty predictable, and the worst you'll get is coffee grinds. There's very little likelihood of an errant tampon or dirty diaper.

Once the trio has finished eating, Channing bends over and goes through the bag for one last search. Putting his arm in deeper this time, he gingerly feels around and pulls out a pastry filled with custard and covered in berries, then a second, then a third. He passes one to Flo, and, once again, offers the last to Miles. It's got fewer berries than the rest, but Miles snaps it up.

As he's done everywhere else we've been until now, Miles stands back a foot or so while Channing or Flo rummage through a bag. He watches rather than takes the initiative, and it's obvious from early on that he is outclassed. This is okay with Miles. You get the feeling he'd prefer Channing and Flo do the looking anyway.

"I'm not very good at this," he says. "I'm low income and all, but I'm lazy. I usually just live off peanut butter and bagels."

Miles, until we run into the more garbage-savvy duo of Flo and Channing, is meant to be my guide for the night. The arrangement we made several days earlier was to meet in

Washington Square at ten P.M., that being the time when the smaller takeouts in the area start closing and the garbage gets put out, often along with some leftover food—unsold or half eaten.

Miles arrives fifteen minutes late. He comes careering through Washington Square on a red bicycle, narrowly missing several members of a troupe dressed in white who are finishing off a performance of *A Midsummer Night's Dream*. He has cycled from Queens, across the Fifty-ninth Street Bridge, and three miles down Fifth Avenue. The bicycle, he explains, besides being his sole form of transport (he can't afford subways and buses) is also a good way of getting around when you're looking for food. You can cover more distance than on foot, and you can carry things that are too heavy to walk with. Miles's friend Juan goes one better, tying a small trailer to his bike to put the food in.

Goochi Sushi on Eighth Street is our first stop, and for several good reasons. It is nearby, only a few blocks from Washington Square, and it is a takeout that usually has left-overs.

"Sometimes they put the food at the top of the bag, so it's easier to find," Miles says as we set off, his voice eager with anticipation. "They know we'll be looking for it."

By the time we reach Goochi and he goes through the first bag, it's clear that someone has gotten there before him. It is only twenty-five minutes after closing, but the bag has already been claimed. I don't realize it then, but Goochi is a place where you have to literally stand in line for the garbage. Several nights later I will see a man with a trolley outside the store, patiently waiting for the food to be thrown out a full forty-five minutes before closing.

Miles, who has been looking forward to an alternative to peanut butter and bagels the whole night, is visibly disappointed. For several minutes he looks up and down Eighth Street, and I soon figure out that it's because he has no idea where to go next. My guide into the world of food collecting is an ingenue. His face suddenly lights up when he sees two friendly faces cycling toward us. It's Channing and Flo.

"Hey," Miles calls out, "I didn't know you were in town."

In the milk crate on the back of Channing's bike, there's something familiar sticking out from between some old newspaper. It's take-out sushi: two trays of California rolls, four hand rolls, and one tray of nigiri sushi. It turns out that Channing and Flo were already at Goochi, then went on to a grocery store, where they were less successful. Miles asks if we can team up with them.

"Sure," Channing says. Flo looks at me suspiciously for a few moments—she seems to think that I might somehow be involved with law enforcement, ready to bust them at any minute—but finally she nods that it's okay.

Their next stop, a few blocks west, is a branch of Au Bon Pain. About two dozen garbage bags lie scattered outside the store, most of them see-through, making their contents easy to identify at a glance. Two of them each contain a large cardboard tray full of doughnuts, Danish, pains au chocolat, Copenhagens, and croissants. Flo grabs an empty Krispy Kreme box and starts lining it with pastries. Miles follows her lead and does the same.

When Flo sees me watching her cram as much confectionery as possible into the box, she looks embarrassed. "These aren't *all* for us," she explains. "There are more people at home."

Miles shoves a pain au chocolat into his mouth as he

continues filling his box. He is sweating profusely, what with the evening air being so warm and him having ridden from Long Island City. His clothes are paint splattered and smell, which could be from all the exercise he's done but also from not having been washed for a long time. Miles is twenty-six, boyish looking at times, handsome in a tousled kind of way. If you didn't know better, he could pass for one of the New York University students ambling by on the sidewalk. He seems distant most of the time, as if he's dim-witted or disinterested. He is neither.

Until a few months earlier, Miles worked as a messenger, delivering videos on the Upper East Side. On his rounds, he would collect things off the street—canvas and frames mostly, seeing he's an aspiring artist—but he left all of it behind in his former apartment, which he vacated at the beginning of the summer.

"I gave up the job and the apartment at the same time. I realized I was just working to pay the rent."

Now he paints full-time and moves from house to house, from acquaintance to acquaintance, into anyplace where they'll put him up. While the weather is still good, he sleeps on the roof of a tenement building in Queens.

Sometimes Miles steals food, or rather, he steals peanut butter. Whenever he buys a bag of bagels, he will bury a jar of Jif under his shirt. He goes to one supermarket chain in particular because the narrow aisles and the poorly placed cameras make it easier to pilfer there without being caught. He doesn't brag about stealing—in fact, he seems a bit embarrassed by it—but it helps him get by. If he can avoid paying for something, he does. When he travels to his parents, in Louisiana, he jumps a freight train to get there. He has crossed

America jumping freight trains. He tries to convince me to write about the people who jump freight trains instead of the people who collect food.

"Or the circus," he adds. "Write about the circus."

Something about the way Miles says "the circus" makes me want to ask more. He hardly seems like the kind of person who could afford to, or who would even want to, go to a performance of Ringling Bros. But before I have a chance to question him further, Flo breaks in.

"Try not to rip the bags!" she instructs everyone. She turns to me to explain. "The store can get fined if there's a mess."

"Yes," Channing adds, smirking, "we're protecting our future."

There is always a theatrical tone in Channing's voice, as if he's making fun of someone, even himself. This habit, along with his perpetual grin, makes it hard ever to take him seriously. Even as he sinks his teeth into a cream-centered chocolate doughnut, he pulls a face and acts out his delight.

"Mmmm. Scrum-diddlee-umptious."

When Flo finally places the filled-up Krispy Kreme box in the milk crate on her bike, she does so carefully, to avoid it getting squashed. Then she proposes the route they should take for the rest of the evening and which stores they should go to. Out of her satchel she produces a crudely drawn map of downtown, on which there are about two dozen black squares with the words "Free Food Here" written next to them. On the reverse side of the paper are the names of the stores and what kind of food you can expect to be thrown away. Most of them are pastry and candy stores. Flo says she tries to balance junk food with things that are healthy.

"Our friend Appolonia made this," she says, holding out

the map. At the bottom of one side it says, '*Copy this and pass on.*' "I've never used it before. Usually I just go to the places I know."

"This is research at its very best," adds Channing, grinning.

"We should get to Nirvana soon," Flo suggests. "They put out their food an hour ago already." To encourage everyone, she adds, "They might even have tofu."

Flo and Channing set the pace, heading deeper into the East Village, which is where they do most of their hunting. They call what they do Dumpster diving, even though a Dumpster is seldom, if ever, involved. Garbage bags, either black or see-through, are what they're after, and only those that are situated outside restaurants or food stores. But these kids wouldn't be mistaken for black-bag people; they collect with almost painstaking care and work not singly but in a group.

In tonight's group, Flo quickly assumes the position of leader, even though it's Channing who is always in the lead. Miles, meanwhile, is happy to tag along, like a loyal supporter. Channing and Flo claim to be the best collectors in their house, telling me, almost in unison, that they also like doing it the most. They aren't boyfriend and girlfriend, but they work well together.

Flo is twenty-two, wears a black halter top that leaves her stomach exposed and bulging slightly over her knee-length pants. Her hair is done in girlish plaits, and her legs are unshaved. She sometimes has a job, either doing lights and sound in theater or painting houses. She comes from Massachusetts and lives in an apartment with Channing and a group of other people for perhaps a month at a time when she is in the city, then leaves again. She says I am welcome to refer to her as Flo when I write about her, which I find odd given her suspicion of me, but then she adds that Flo isn't her real name anyway.

Channing, on the other hand, doesn't mind me using his real name. "You can also call me Wonderdog," he says, then barks. He is nineteen and he sometimes sounds uncannily like Homer Simpson. His sideburns are bushy, his skin peachy soft—half child, half adult—and he wears a dirty T-shirt, braces, and jeans cut off raggedly at the knee. On the back of his right calf is a big round blue tattoo with the words *Gatoch Fietsen!* (Go ride your bike!) written in the center. His sinewy legs pump up and down on the pedals as he rides like a maniac through the nighttime traffic, and within seconds of leaving Au Bon Pain he is way ahead of everyone else.

Between the bicycle he transforms into a projectile, darting in and out of traffic, and a face he flexes into a mishmash of expressions, it's not surprising to learn that he works as a cycling, accordion-playing clown in a traveling circus. (It's the circus that Miles was referring to.) He collects even when he travels, but Flo says she does it only in New York.

"There's so much here, it's hard not to," she says. "Today I paid for one meal, was bought one meal, and got one meal off the street."

"In lots of places you can't do it," Channing says, then almost spits out the reason. "Trash compactors!"

Flo agrees. "Trash compactors are evil."

As he cycles, Channing constantly performs, either singing pieces of opera by Verdi or reciting lines from various skits he's acted in, one of which is about a man named Mr. Monsanto. Gibes, funny faces, caustic remarks—his performance is nonstop. All of it remains strictly verbal until, outside a store

called Nirvana, Flo dares him to play a prank, which is when
his act becomes physical. Having pulled a discarded banana
from a garbage bag, he hears Flo repeat her challenge.

"Do the banana!"

He looks back at her, then arches an eyebrow.

"You want me to do the banana?"

Without waiting for an answer, he peels the fruit slowly,
lets the flesh fall away, walks to a nearby restaurant, and
places the skin facedown at the entrance. He does it very
slowly and dramatically—he knows that we are watching his
every move—then comes away smiling. Suddenly he mimics
someone falling, arms flailing, which happened the last time
he played the same prank.

Channing doesn't appear to see anything wrong with his
actions. He saunters back to the garbage bags and continues
searching. Life outside the circus is also a circus, it seems, and
garbage can as easily be a prop as it can be dinner.

Nirvana is a health-food store. Flo and Channing like health-
food stores even more than candy stores, or at least it sounds
that way. One particular health food gets mentioned so many
times and with such reverence, in fact, that it seems to be the
standard by which all other products are measured. Soy milk.

"You hardly ever find soy milk," Flo says.

Miles doesn't hear her because he has been distracted by a
partly eaten portion of curried vegetables. The bags he has
gone through, in his distinctive halfhearted manner, lie to one
side of him. As Miles contemplates the curry—to eat or not
to eat—Flo and Channing continue their methodical search:
They take a bag, open it, fan a hand across the topmost
contents, reach through the surface, snake their way through

to the deepest corners, knock the bag gently against the sidewalk to hear if there's anything solid at the bottom they might have missed, close the bag, put it aside, take another.

"It's worth going through old fruit and vegetables," says Flo. "I once found a container of vegan chocolate that way."

Channing lifts a packet he has retrieved and holds it up to the sky like a trophy. "Waffle mix," he cries out, then adds dramatically, "Ooh, waffle!"

The people walking along the sidewalk skirt around the threesome, which in itself isn't odd. Most people give collectors a wide berth, because they're scared or don't exactly know what to expect of them. It's the eternal bum-lunatic conclusion. But nowhere does it seem more out of place than in the East Village, full of university students and twentysomethings out on a Friday night, who bear a striking resemblance to Miles, Flo, and Channing—the same age, the same demeanor, and the same clothes—except the collectors look grungy out of necessity not choice. Their IQs, I will also learn, are as good as any university student's, possibly better.

"Sometimes people see what we're doing and say, eee-yew, how gross," says Flo, pulling a single leaf of chard out of a bag, inspecting it, and putting it to one side. "Other times they offer to buy us a meal. We just say, no thanks, we have plenty of food here. Outside Doughboy one night, we found a whole load of bread. We offered some to a couple who walked past. At first they said no, but when they saw how delicious the bread looked, they took some."

Having finished with her own bags, and without making too much of a fuss about it, Flo double-checks the ones Miles has already done. She runs her hand through some discarded vegetables on top, and without too much effort she comes across a full bottle of juice. Miles, who is still inspecting the curried vegetables, blushes.

"Oh, I didn't see that," he says. As Flo pulls out a second bottle, and a third, he admits what's been obvious from the start. "I'm not very good at this. I'm learning from these guys."

After another five minutes all their finds from Nirvana are laid out on the sidewalk: a leaf of chard, three bottles of juice, six tubs of yogurt (one without a cap but still sealed), a packet of waffle mix, a big bottle of lemonade (whose cap is damaged but unbroken), six packets of tofu (which they will have to eat by tomorrow because they don't have a fridge), a pack of fennel-flavored biscuits, five bags of apple-cinnamon mini–rice cakes, a bag of almond pieces, a bag of smashed pistachios, and several tubs of seitan.

"What's seitan?" asks Miles, studying the wrinkled chunks of protein. "It looks like fake meat."

"It's bad for you," Flo cautions him, sounding motherly. "It's got wheat in it, and lots of people shouldn't eat wheat."

Miles takes the seitan anyway.

They deliberate for several minutes over five packets of mortadella slices. Should they them or not? They are hungry, but they are vegetarian. Is it bad to throw away good food, even if it is meat?

"No one at the house eats meat, do they?" Flo asks. Channing isn't sure. They decide to leave the mortadella slices on top of the bags for someone else to find. Once again, they offer to split their booty with Miles, but he shakes his head. He's happy with his pastries and the seitan. Before we leave, he tosses the curried vegetables.

The four of us course along Third Avenue, once again riding against the heavy Friday night traffic. We could go in the direction of the vehicles, but instead Channing takes us east on Ninth Street, which flows west, and then south on Third Avenue, which goes north. It's almost like a challenge, a dare, an escapade, as if to say: Why can't scrounging for food be as wild as clubbing on a Friday night?

Channing zigzags through the cars and keeps losing everyone else, but that doesn't matter. He and Flo have already agreed that they would meet up at Doughboy, after Channing mentioned that they needed bread. It is the only item on their unwritten shopping list. Everything else is gathered simply because it's available and it's edible.

Doughboy is closed by the time the last of us pulls up, and two men are sitting on a bench outside. A single small bag on the sidewalk suggests the pickings won't be good.

"No bread tonight," one of the men tells Channing before he can even get off his bike. His face falls. They had a good haul here on their last visit a week ago, and he was expecting the same tonight.

"Try tomorrow," the man suggests.

"You'll have bread then?" Channing asks.

"Maybe."

Encouraged by that vague promise, Channing pushes down on the pedals and speeds along Fourth Street, once again in the wrong direction. The Amalfi, a candy store on Stanton Street, is the next and last stop. Channing goes through the first bag and finds nothing except a small triangle of chocolate. You'd think that someone who had been known to find five-gallon drums of chocolate wouldn't bother with this morsel, but he does. Like Dave, the sludger, he's never too proud. He offers it to the others first, and after they decline, he eats it by himself. He carries on digging, even after Flo gives up, and eventually finds a bag of dried pears and at least two handfuls of sugared square jellies. Everyone starts eating the candy as if they hadn't already had enough doughnuts, Danish, and chocolate-covered strawberries.

The milk crates on Flo's and Channing's bikes are almost full by now, and since their apartment is only a few blocks away, Flo suggests they go home and drop them off. On the way, she reminds the others of a place she's heard about that sometimes throws away slices of pizza—"natural vegetarian pizza," she adds, the voice of encouragement—but only after one A.M. Everyone repeats the word *pizza*, making it sound quite magical, better than sushi and candy, and possibly even better than soy milk.

Channing and Flo live on the sixth floor of a walk-up on Rivington Street, on the Lower East Side. Or rather, they eat their meals and hang out there. They usually sleep on the roof. Six of them are squatting in the apartment of a guy named Sanjay, who lets them live there for as long as they need to.

The apartment, on this humid summer night, smells sickly sweet. It could be from food that has been left lying around for too long without refrigeration, or it could be the bath, which is in the kitchen and is half full of used soapy water. The combination of smells (old food, old bathwater) initially makes me feel like gagging, and the place looks tidy but poorly cleaned. Cockroaches crawl along the wall, over the stove, into the sink.

Everyone in the apartment collects food, which they do mostly at night. Since Flo and Channing like the job so much, however, the others have been relying on the twosome for the last few weeks. But that arrangement will be ending soon:

Flo's month in the city is almost over and Channing is going on tour.

As Flo enters the apartment, she announces their arrival, "Hey, food! Come and get it!"

"For the doughnuts make us strong!" a female voice replies singsongily from the balcony.

Two women enter the kitchen. They are in their twenties, and both wear black slacks and tank tops. One of them, Saskia, carries a guitar. "I'm soooo hungry," she says. Her friend's name is Iona. They circle the table, eye out the food, and then both go for the same item—the sushi.

"That is the one thing that makes New York unique," Iona says. "The sushi. You don't get this off the street anywhere else in the world."

Iona has collected food in London, Prague, and Quebec City. In London, she and her friends got their vegetables off the floor of the fresh produce market near Covent Garden. When she says that, I suddenly realize I've seen her, Flo, Channing, and all the food collectors before. It was in a documentary called *The Gleaners and I*. They might have spoken French in the movie, and might have braided their hair, but they sounded the same, political and a bit angry at the world. They were also equally beautiful, something the director, Agnès Varda, found it important to comment on, especially given the origin of their Dumpster diet.

In the movie, Varda traced the custom of gleaning back to the days of Jean-François Millet's famous painting, when women used to pick up whatever was left behind by the harvesters. Varda went around France in search of modern-day gleaners and found housewives collecting the apples passed over by the official pickers, men knocking apart TVs to collect the copper in the back, and a man living in a derelict trailer who chose what he wanted from mountains of potatoes that had been deemed too big or not good enough for the stores. The group of beautiful twentysomethings had recently been charged in court for writing graffiti on a supermarket exterior after raiding its Dumpsters for food, an incident that left them even angrier than usual. The gleaner who most impressed Varda, though, was a man with a master's degree who lived in a city shelter, where he taught French to immigrants from Africa, and ate a very choice diet from the floor of marketplaces, making sure to consume lots of fruit and vegetables.

Everyone at Rivington Street has seen *The Gleaners and I*, even though movies are a luxury they can ill afford and it played at only one location in the city when it was released. The character they relate to best was a man in his thirties who despite having a full-time job had, for the past ten years, eaten out of Dumpsters as a kind of personal protest against mankind's wastefulness and abuse of nature, evidenced in disasters like oil spillages at sea. They remark on how outspoken and militant he was. They like that.

The food collectors, you see, are more than just collectors, a fact that Miles had alerted me to even before we met in Washington Square. He told me over the phone, "Maybe when we go out, you can meet the anarchists." He didn't elaborate, but he didn't have to. By the time we reach Rivington Street, I have seen and heard enough—from Flo's unshaved legs, to Miles's habit of hopping freight trains, to practically everyone's desire to attend Burning Man, the weeklong gathering of experimental living that takes place annually in the Black Rock Desert of Nevada—to suggest lives that are if not anarchic, then at least as unusual as their eating habits. There is something both annoying and refreshing about this. They behave recklessly (going against the traffic, tossing banana peels where they are most likely to cause injury, not paying rent), but their actions aren't entirely thoughtless. They eat out of the trash in order not to waste, and at the same time they manage to maintain a balanced diet. They care for the world and for their own good health. Even when they steal food, they make a point of avoiding the mom-and-pop stores and target the large chain supermarkets instead. And they are careful never to mess when they collect, just in case someone might get fined afterward.

Out of all the residents on Rivington Street, the most politically vocal is Iona. All the cities where she has collected food and squatted—besides London, Prague, and Quebec City, she has spent time in Seattle and Milan—have something in common. Each one has, in recent years, hosted a meeting of one or other organization that symbolizes much of what the food collectors find reprehensible about the world today: the G8 countries, the Summit of the Americas, the World Bank, the IMF, and the World Trade Organization.

Iona, along with hundreds of thousands of youngsters like her, went to those cities to demonstrate. When she wasn't holding a placard, she was helping cook food for protesters, under the auspices of Food Not Bombs. Described in its own material as one of the fastest-growing revolutionary movements in North America, Food Not Bombs was started in 1980 by antinuclear activists, has no leaders, works on a volunteer basis, and is aligned with groups like Earth First! and In Defense of Animals. All the food it cooks is found on the streets.

"I always thought it was Food Nut Bombs," jokes Channing,

but no one laughs. By this stage, he has shouldered his accordion and plays whatever tune comes to mind.

"It's a very loose organization," Iona explains. "People will recognize the name, whatever city you're in. You'll put up a sign and it'll say, Food Not Bombs serving out of such-and-such a place and time, and people will come."

"It's usually vegan," adds Flo, the meat-and-wheat-hater, "sometimes vegetarian. There are other groups that do the same thing, except they travel around and serve food. The Seeds of Peace Kitchen and Everybody's Kitchen."

Whenever Flo interjects, it's as if she is trying to prove her importance in the group and display her knowledge of their culture. When I first mention the word *anarchist,* she shakes her head in disapproval. She insists that they aren't anarchists, they aren't anything. They abhor categories.

"It's not like we've gotten together and said this is our philosophy. We all have our own personal philosophy."

"That's what makes us strong," Iona says, "what unifies us. Some of us lead partly normal lives. Some of us never go back into mainstream culture. It's a reactionary culture. All of us look at what is happening in America, in most of the world, and we say, "This is perverted, nasty, ridiculous, immature; everything is wrong." She pauses. "It's consumerism."

"And capitalism," Flo says.

"And globalization," adds Miles.

Everyone turns back to Iona, not only because she is sitting in the middle of the room, right next to the table where the food is laid out, but also because she is the closest thing they have to a leader. In the same way that Flo leads the group outdoors, Iona does so indoors. And it's obvious why. She has traveled the world, has attended the demon-

4

strations, and can talk with authority about the issues of the day. It also doesn't hurt that she's gorgeous, a dead ringer for the actress Julia Ormond, except her hair is cropped and blonde. The more she talks, the more vociferous she becomes.

"We say, 'Efficient—bottom line,' that's bullshit. We're people and we need to have people being people. That's why I'd never call myself an activist. Because that's saying it's my profession, that's all I do. No, I'm a person. Part of being a person is being socially conscious."

Iona litters her stories with jargon and things she has probably read in pamphlets, but they're related with as much conviction as her own experiences. In between her reflections on running a Food Not Bombs kitchen out of a squat in Prague, she throws in something about Henry Ford's assembly line having infiltrated the average American life and people no longer being people but cogs in a big machine.

"Our world is erratic by nature," she says, looking at her friends around the room and describing a world that sounds very much like the one Sarah found herself in thirty-five years earlier. "It's kind of an underground, a counterculture. It's political, it's artistic, it's a squatter world, and it Dumpster dives. We're against mainstream culture, yes, but also against consumerism. Culture today is based on producing and spending more and more at an increasing level because that's the only way a market can grow. But in doing so, it wastes more and more resources.

"People throw out nice futons, nice clothes, good food—sushi—because they have been told to consume more and more. It's so ingrained that it doesn't occur to them that by throwing this stuff out they are also wasting wood and basic resources.

We try to consume as little as possible. There's no need to buy anything."

Iona turns to the guitarist Saskia, who is busy eating a doughnut now that the sushi is finished.

"Saskia just found this incredible outfit, a cashmere sweater that hadn't been used, and she wore it to a job interview. You don't even have to go to secondhand stores. You just go and find it in the trash."

"Or we make what we need," says Flo.

Someone holds up a coffee cup that's been fashioned out of a glass jar and a piece of tin for a handle. Flo points to her waist, where her keys are held together by an old shower curtain ring. The artists among them—and there are several besides Miles—find cardboard and paint rather than buy it new.

"We don't want to take away from the environment," says Iona. "It's been raped enough already."

The idea of organized politics is anathema to most of the food collectors, although Iona worked on Ralph Nader's 2000 presidential campaign. Nader had proved his good faith by leading the coalition of protesters against the WTO gathering in Seattle in 1999, but you can hear from the muttering around the room that support for him isn't unanimous.

"There are people who don't want to work within the political system," Iona says. "Some want to work within the cultural system, but others say, 'Fuck America, fuck you guys; we're going to fuck shit up because you guys are ridiculous.'"

Channing comes back into the room, now playing his accordion so loudly that it's hard to hear Iona.

"Quiet!" she shouts.

Lowering the volume, but still playing, Channing tries to be conciliatory and to pick up where Iona left off.

"And then there are some of us who fuck things up by doing shows."

"Yeah," says Miles.

He grins at me across the room. Finally, the circus.

"It's not Ringling Brothers with a big tent," Miles adds, in case I had any doubt.

"Ringling's an institution," adds Channing. His comment is not meant to be a criticism, but it sounds like one.

The circuses that get mentioned have names that Channing the jokester could have made up. Circus Amok and Cyclown. According to a brochure someone hands me, Circus Amok brings "funny, queer, caustic and sexy, political one-ring spectacles to diverse neighborhoods . . ." It offers something old and a lot that's new, a combination of acrobats, puppetry, gender-bending performance art, and some social commentary. Which explains how Channing landed up in a skit about the fictitious Mr. Monsanto, an unlikable genetic engineer who played around with animal DNA until he ended up creating a plaid kangaroo. Cyclown's strength is, as its name implies, clowns and cyclists, and its members spent a recent summer touring refugee camps, schools, and orphanages across Eastern Europe and Palestine.

"People think they're going to a real circus," says Channing, obviously loving the subtle deceit, "but then they take their seats and—zap!—we have them. We can pummel them with new ideas."

"It's like a circus, but without the animals," adds Miles.

"There's dogs," Channing corrects him. "They just don't perform; they tag along."

"It's an extravaganza, a drunken blur, crazy," says Miles, much more carried away with the circus than with collecting.

"It's medieval. It's like gypsies entertaining people only with what they have in their caravans."

Most of the collectors on Rivington Street have worked in the circus at one time or another. Channing's unicycle is parked in the hallway outside their apartment, Iona has been an acrobat, Miles has done publicity, and Flo has worked the lights. Iona says that the circuses were, in fact, born out of their street culture.

"When people aren't Dumpster diving, they are busking to make a living," she adds.

Demonstrators in Prague, for instance, were taught by a group called Initiative Against Economic Globalisation, or Inpeg, not only about making human chains, first aid, tree climbing, and communicating with the media, but also about street theater. And "theater," in this community, could mean just about anything. Iona mentions a circus whose freak show doesn't exploit people's physical peculiarities, but other ones. Among the featured performers are a woman who can swing a six-pack from her clitoris, a man who carries out self-fellatio on a bed of nails, and a transsexual who bites a live wire to light a bulb between her legs.

Everyone in the room shrieks with delight at the mention of the freaks.

"They're wildcats," says Miles.

Flo screws up her face in disgust. "They're dirty."

"Oh, they're such nice people," Channing sings and then pumps his accordion for effect.

Flo, who has repeatedly been trying to remind everyone that it is almost one o'clock—time to go in search of pizza— suddenly gets caught up in the talk about the counterculture, the circus, the freaks.

"And then there's the Radical Cheerleaders," she says.

The Radical Cheerleaders are a loose-knit group that, for a decade or more, has been leading chants and songs at protests and rallies, many of which have become war cries for the disenchanted. The cheers deal with everything from NAFTA, to abortion, to sweatshops, to the degrading nature of women's magazines, to the death penalty, to immigration. The last subject inspires Flo to start up a cheer, and everyone joins in.

"Eeny meeny miney mo-oh-oh / To the border here we go / Will they let you cross? Hell, no / That's because you're from Mexico / If you have fine brown skin / Then crossing is a sin / Just want to see some kin? / I-N-S won't let you in / Eeny meeny miney mo-oh-oh."

The food has slowly been nibbled at throughout the evening. Once the sushi is finished and more than half the Krispy Kreme box of pastries and cakes has been eaten, a packet each of tofu and fennel rice cakes get opened. Putting a doughnut in his mouth, Channing moves into the next room, where he tries to pick up a tune Saskia is playing on her guitar. As she sings, several of the words from the chorus reach us, and the subject of the melody couldn't be more perfect.

"It's the Dumpster-diving song!" Saskia says.

Most of the people in the room don't know all the words, but they know the chorus by heart. Not a single Dumpster has figured in their collecting tonight, but it remains a symbol of their antiestablishment lifestyle as well as a declaration of their faith. It signifies both what's wrong with the world and what they can do to help save it. It is also about freedom—train-hopping, circus-going, Dumpster-diving freedom.

Saskia agrees to play the song only if everyone joins her, so they gather around Flo, who holds a book of Radical Cheers. The melody it gets sung to is, quite appropriately, "Solidarity Forever."

"Is there ought we have in common with the greedy para- sites / Besides that we eat out of their Dumpster every night? / Is there anything left for us? / Open the lid and take a bite / For the doughnuts make us strong."

During each chorus, Channing moves about the room, pumping his accordion.

"Dumpster diving forever, Dumpster diving forever / Dumpster diving forever. For the doughnuts make us strong."

Several singers lose the beat every now and then, or Channing plays too fast and puts them off, but they rally for every chorus, almost shouting in their eagerness.

"They have wasted untold millions and they waste more every day / While the workers keep producing, they keep throwing it away / But the freegans [vegans who get free food] are uniting and we vow to never pay / For the doughnuts make us strong."

Channing comes back to the group for the next verse.

"We may be industry-dependent, hypocritical leeches / But while you work to buy carob organic brownies, we'll be swimming at the beaches / And when 'green' consumerism dies we'll be making freegan speeches / For the doughnuts make us sick."

When they're finished singing, Flo looks at the clock on the wall. It has just gone one A.M., and once again she is anxious about the pizzas that might be out on First Avenue. Channing, in deference to his collecting partner, detaches himself from his accordion and heads for the front door.

"Let's go," he says, and Miles immediately follows him.

"Yay, pizza!" Flo shouts when she sees the reaction. The cry of motivation is like the one she made when she discovered the chocolate-coated strawberries at the start of the evening, except now, after the Radical Cheers, I almost expect her to do a cheerleader routine and spell out the letters P-I-Z-Z-A.

Just as Channing opens the front door, a blond woman in her twenties comes down the hall to the apartment opposite theirs. Dressed in black, she looks as if she is returning home after a night of clubbing. She lives in one of three apartments in the building that have recently been renovated and are being rented out for a small fortune. As the East Village becomes more trendy, people like Channing and Flo are becoming the rarities, and it's hard not to foresee a time when they will have moved on for good.

The blonde and Channing stand face to face, one paying three thousand dollars a month in rent, the other nothing, the two of them, both the same age, representing the two worlds that I have seen brushing past each other the whole evening. I try to imagine how the blonde would react to the Radical Cheerleaders and the six-pack-attached-to-her-clitoris freak and Circus Amok. I'm not even sure she knows that her neighbors live the way they do. Channing breaks the silence.

"Doughnut?" he asks, offering her some of the cast-off pastries.

"Wow," the girl says, lighting up when she sees all the food on the kitchen table, "you guys been having a party?"

Channing doesn't answer but smiles and holds the plate closer to her. After she takes a doughnut and goes into her apartment, he turns to me and becomes serious for the very first time that evening.

"Sometimes it's better not to say where the food comes from.'

chapter 5

the visionaries

At about the same time that Agnès Varda was shooting *The Gleaners and I* in France, another Parisian was shooting a documentary about a gleaner in New York. Jean Barat, an actor and filmmaker with a pre-*Matrix* taste for long black coats, was staying with a friend in the Bowery who lived in the first floor and basement of a brownstone. The apartment had captivated Barat in the past, but this time he wanted to document it.

The opening scene of his short film takes place in a large room—a long, combined kitchen–dining room–living room—and every frame is filled with golden light and warm woods. Two men, one with a shaved head and the other with long hair, sit at a table, drink coffee, and talk, the shaved man occasionally translating so that Barat can understand. But the Parisian is less interested in commentary than in the interior of the apartment.

He starts at (1) a cabinet behind the two men that is so long that only a section of it fits into the frame, and Barat needs to pan the camera to get it all in. Each of the cabinet's display areas—there are eleven in all—is bathed in a soft glow, created in part by (2) exquisitely textured oval shades that cover the lightbulbs. Stretched above the cabinet is (3) a large oil painting done in the style of Chagall of two nudes lying with their legs intertwined.

In the ceiling you can see one side of (4) a large light box, centered with (5) a huge fan. Suddenly there's a close-up of (6) a Mickey Mouse coffee mug held by the shaved man, who says isn't it terrible that everything in America nowadays is made in China. He adds, for Barat's sake, *"Toute ici est fabriqué en Chine. Toute."* Back at the cabinet again, the camera takes in parts of its interior, including (7a) a black-and-white photograph of a young Italian boy at his first Holy Communion kneeling on a strip of fur and (7b) a coarse sculpture in the shape of a bone.

Now near the edge of the dining table, Barat turns upward to (8) a Waterford chandelier, suspended from the center of (9) a three-foot-wide octagon shape in the ceiling that is deep gold at its center and slowly gets brighter as it spreads out, finally splintering into (10) a brilliant starburst. He then moves to the end of the kitchen–dining room–living room and through (11) a wooden archway, down several steps, and into (12) a large room dominated by (13a) several solid wood cabinets and (13b) a seven-foot tower of roughly hewn wooden drawers.

Straight ahead is an empty backyard that's covered in snow. Taking a right turn, Barat descends some steps and passes (14) a painting, a classical rendering of the Last Supper, which hangs next to a small bathroom whose walls are done in (15) a richly textured wallpaper crisscrossed in small trails of filigree.

At the bottom of the stairway is the basement, where (16) thick ten-foot-long wooden shelves recessed into the walls are filled with cassettes, CDs, books, and clothes neatly folded like a store display. Several beds positioned in various parts of the room are covered in different fabrics and cushions, and the way they are surrounded in swathes of netting hung from the ceiling, they each look like a corner of a harem.

Back upstairs, the shaved-headed man is now seated in the middle of a blue bedroom. Above the bed is (17) a window that is as wide as the bed is long, although the view through it is obscured by the interior light reflecting off the panes. Next to (18) the fireplace is (19) a large metal artwork that resembles a meat scale framed on three sides with wood, and on the mantel is (20) an antique of some sort, a curious contraption with rows of lights and letters inscribed on it. As Barat makes his way back to the main room, he passes (21) a second Last Supper, this one very large and modern, with the twelve apostles depicted as naked skinheads.

For his last interior shots, Barat returns to the huge wall cabinet, where the camera lingers over several of the displays, each niche and its contents a tableau backed by (22) richly evocative wallpaper, its design incorporating portraits, stamps, and even some kind of script, although the camera moves too quickly for you to read what it says.

Barat's film is a lot cruder than Varda's and not at all philosophical. There is no title at the start, and it ends just as abruptly, on a snowy street outside the house, with the filmmaker sporting his signature black coat. The film is impersonal and detached, and it could as easily be taken inside some chalet in Bavaria as in an apartment in the Bowery. Barat would later use clips from the movie in a multimedia theatrical show at the summer festival in Avignon, but in neither work do you learn one of the most important details about the house where it was shot, 143 Allen Street. Namely, it had heart. In the vast, often alienating canvas of New York City, it was a warm and inviting address. The dinner table was a gathering mongo

place for home-cooked meals every night of the week, and a fire burned in the two fireplaces throughout the winter. But most of all, it was a place where anyone—yes, anyone, from an artist to a diplomat to a stranger off the street—could be found and was always welcome.

"It was just like a *salon*," says Jeffrey, whose home it was, pronouncing the word the French way.

But in Barat's film most of the shots are curiously devoid of human life, and the camera seems more interested in the setting and the décor, sailing silently across a row of books, resting for a moment on a cat lazing in a corner, zooming in on some purple bubble lights, and then panning across a red wall, a blue ceiling, a white floor. It is *Budget Living* meets *House Beautiful* on film, or Varda sans the philosophy and good editing, and anyone watching it could come away thinking this was the tastefully designed home of a person, a decorator possibly, with a somewhat eclectic taste and a love of dark woods.

Which was exactly Barat's intention. He didn't want to capture what Allen Street, as most visitors liked to call it, was about but what it *was*. As a filmmaker, he admired the fact that the décor was pure artifice, not at all what it seemed. Almost everything in the apartment came from the street, but in being rescued it not only began a new life, it began a life as something else. In the same way that a film can create an illusion, so did Allen Street. In the documentary, what you think you see in practically every shot isn't what you actually see. That's why it's helpful to go through the numbers again.

The shaved-headed man in the film is Jeffrey, the person largely responsible for transforming Allen Street. The long-haired man is his housemate, Sean. Behind them is not a

106

cabinet but (1) seven mahogany doors taken out of a Dumpster in front of a nearby tenement house and jimmied together to look as if they're one. Four of the doors once contained panes, although the glass had been broken when they were packed into the Dumpster. Each of the eleven display areas is bathed in light that is softened not by real shades but by (2) numerous translucent amber fan shells that Jeffrey gathered on the beach at Boca Grande, Florida, and suspended by wire over the bulbs.

Stretched above the make-believe cabinet is (3) a painting that came from the sidewalk. In the ceiling closer to the camera you can see one side of (4) a light box that Jeffrey made from slatted wood that had once been the base of an old wall, a framework he then spanned between two pieces of rescued beam. The (6) Mickey Mouse mug was dug out of a trash can. Inside the cabinet, the ornaments include (7a) a photograph of an old Italian neighbor as a child, one of many keepsakes thrown out when he died, and (7b) not a sculpture that looked like a bone but a real bone.

The (8) chandelier, along with the (5) fan, was one of the few things in Allen Street that was bought, as was most of the hardware needed to put the house together. Around it the (9) octagon was made of plywood, all of which splinters into (10) a starburst Jeffrey created by cutting hundreds of triangular shapes out of letters he had written but never sent, then pasting them onto the ceiling and shellacking them. Halfway into covering the ceiling, he ran out of letters, which was when he noticed the shape he'd made so far. He left it that way. On the periphery of the starburst, he contrived a basketweave effect by painstakingly interlacing narrow pieces of wood.

To create the (11) two archways, Jeffrey removed two

mismatched sets of French doors and replaced them with beams
taken from a Dumpster on Grand Street. Beyond the doors
there had been an outside porch protected by a second-floor
balcony, and then the garden. The balcony was rotting when
Jeffrey moved in, so he tore it down and built (12) a large
room. With the good leftover wood from the balcony, which
was teak, he made (13a & b) pieces of furniture that one
designer who saw them described as North Italian in feeling—
"modern yet crusty"—and told Jeffrey he should be making
them professionally. "I could easily see his cabinets and shelves
in a Joe Durso apartment," he said, "or in a slick modern
apartment."

Out of the garbage that their Chinese neighbors regularly
threw into the garden, Jeffrey saved, among other things, a
stuffed porcupine doll. It was placed in the cabinet, alongside
the Italian boy at Communion, a bronze of a male nude (given
to Allen Street by a visitor), a huge clamshell (also given), a
Mickey Mantle commemorative plate (found), and a small oil
of a Little Lord Fauntleroy look-alike (also found).

The (14) Last Supper, like most of the paintings in Allen
Street, was rescued. In the nearby bathroom, Jeffrey removed
the sheetrock and exposed (15) several layers of old peeling
wallpaper, which he left unrepaired, although he added spack-
ling to the edges to prevent the layers from peeling any further,
and then he shellacked everything.

The stairs he made so that you didn't have to leave the
apartment to get to the basement. There were no cupboards
downstairs, so (16) ten-foot-long beams from a construction
site were recessed into the wall to create shelf space. Shoe
boxes doubled as drawers. Fabrics and drapes were hung from
the ceiling to create sleeping quarters when they were needed,

for Allen Street was a place where guests were welcome not only to dine but also to spend a few days, if not a few months.

"We had this revolving-door policy," says Jeffrey. "We knew enough people who were young, bohemian, artist types, so we would often have someone who would come and stay."

There was Hamid the Algerian and his girlfriend from Paris; the grandson of the ex-president of Syria; Pedro the designer; two Italian astrologers; Cazi from Burundi; a dancer from Washington, D.C.; a banker from Paris; and Eric Dahan, a journalist with *Liberation* who has been described as "the Michael Musto of French newspapers." When Dahan wrote about a trip to New York, during which he stayed at Allen Street, he described the basement as Ali Baba's Cavern.

Some of the guests added things they'd found or created, from the Chagall-ish nudes to the (21) skinhead Last Supper, specially painted to fit a large wall. Other people donated things they didn't want, and as such Allen Street became the recipient of items that might otherwise have landed on a sidewalk or in a thrift store.

"It was a house that people gave to," says Jeffrey. "Most of our friends, middle class and upper middle class, came from a society that has no one to give things to if they have no more use for them. We were givable."

Whether something was found or given—the piece of pine here, the oak floorboards left over from a Nautica display there, a car stereo—Jeffrey made a point of celebrating it. The half-eaten bone thrown at him by an angry guest had such a lovely shape that he nailed it to the kitchen wall. "Every time I looked at it, I remembered that incident." The oil of the nudes was deliberately left unrepaired, with a big hole in the thigh of the larger woman, in memory of the person who'd brought it home. When a piece of wood that Jeffery had wanted to use on the bathroom was drawn on with a Magic Marker by a crackhead who'd been hanging out at the house, Jeffrey highlighted it. At first he was angry when he heard what had been done, but after seeing it, he was enchanted. "It looked like beautiful oriental calligraphy. When I rebuilt the bathroom, I made it a feature."

The blue bedroom on the first floor was created when Jeffrey built half a wall and placed on top of it (17) a French door that was turned sideways, so that it looked like a window. The (18) fireplace was found, as was (19) the meat scale, which he surrounded in found beams in order to set it off. A (20) contraption he picked up off the sidewalk outside the Plaza-Athénée in Paris also became an ornament, although Jeffrey learned only much later that it was a maid caller, used in the olden days to summon the servants in a hotel.

The (22) wallpaper in the faux cabinet wasn't wallpaper but a salmagundi of paper cuttings: news headlines, then-and-now pictures of the cat-eyed socialite Jocelyne Wildenstein, pieces of a board game, photos of Junior Vasquez, postage stamps on envelopes, and numerous yellowing letters. If you freeze-frame Barat's film, some of the letters can be read, and they say things like "It sucks to be you" and "Love you hate me today." The letters are all signed by Billy Jarecki.

Allen Street would never have looked the way it did if Jeffrey hadn't met Billy Jarecki. It was because of him that Jeffrey began to view objects, and then to use them, in a way he previously would have found unimaginable. The stuffed toy as ornament, the fan shells as lampshades, the meat scale as embellishment; the paintings purposely left unrepaired; and the peeling wallpaper preserved, its wear and tear highlighted instead of covered up.

"I don't think he ever would have had that aesthetic without having been exposed to me," says Billy, who also lived in Allen Street for a while. "Jeffrey was like my customers. He saw that it was okay to see things slightly differently."

Many New Yorkers would probably forgo the extremes of Allen Street, such as the desiccated bone as an objet d'art or the harem look in the basement, but they would nevertheless know who Billy Jarecki is. For Jeffrey isn't the only person whom Billy influenced in such a fundamental way, but he is one of the few to have seriously followed Billy's passion of collecting off the street.

Billy started collecting in the early 1970s, when he was studying art at Cooper Union. I can imagine that he crossed paths with Sarah back then, the one looking for furniture, the other for anything he could use in his artwork. Billy was carrying on a tradition that dated back at least to the Surrealists' use of objets trouvés, and to artists like Marcel Duchamp and Picasso, whose famous sculpture *The Goat* consisted of an old basket, two jugs, some carboard, a palm leaf, a tin, and bits of wood and metal, most of which he got from a rubbish dump near his studio. Among the artists collecting on the streets of New York in the 1970s was Jean-Michel Basquiat.

"We all did it as students," Billy says. "My route every day was the same: the garbage, Canal Street, and then New York Central, an arts supply store. I saw everything I found on the street as a raw material to be recycled in some way or another. That's not a new idea—people do it all the time. But back then, I don't think there were too many people seeing the stuff I was collecting in the same way."

His raw materials included Styrofoam, dishwasher racks, and empty cheese boxes. A fourth item, wooden planks, didn't really qualify as garbage, even though the wood was, at least technically, lying on the street. Roadwork construction at the time was covered not in metal sheets but in strips of wood. So Billy and his friends would go out late at night and steal them. They would leave behind enough wood to cover the ditches and then take what they had gathered back to the workshop.

"We couldn't possibly afford the wood. And believe me, it was fabulous wood. We knew what we were doing wasn't right, but we thought it was okay seeing it was for the sake of art."

The Styrofoam Billy would "deconstruct," especially the large pieces customarily used for packing household appliances, melting them down with solvents and then painting them. Out of the dishwasher racks, whose shapes and colors attracted him most, he made sculptures. But it was the empty cheese boxes that were his true favorite, and they all came from the same place, Murray's Cheese Market.

"Murray's was *the* place to buy cheese back then, and they had the best garbage. I had a fixation on the boxes, especially the wheel boxes. There were also great wooden crates with metal latches on them. Even the papers the cheeses came wrapped in were beautiful—waxy, heavy, textured. In theory the boxes were for artwork, but I just kept them as containers. I was insatiable, and I eventually had a basement full of cheesy-smelling crates and boxes."

Anyone who's never looked at a lone block of Styrofoam or a leftover dishwasher rack as a collectible or an item with which to decorate a home might view Billy's taste as just plain weird. To him, though, these items weren't any different from something you might buy at a flea market. Your reaction in each case is exactly the same: You see something, you want it, and even though you might not know where it comes from or what it's used for, you take it.

Billy recalls once being at the flea market on Grand Street, which had as many kinds of vendors as Twenty-sixth Street does today, and seeing a ball-shaped piece of glass for sale. Without having a clue what it was, he bought it, took it home, and turned it into a vase. Only much later did he discover that it was actually a sock darner.

"It's the same with things you pick up off the street," he says. "And sometimes they turn out to be things you can use."

Billy and his partner at the time, Tom Pritchard, opened a plant store in the West Village called Madderlake, after the muddy, dark red pigments madder and lake. Within a year the store had been discovered by Anna Wintour, now the editor in chief of *Vogue*, who described it in *New York* magazine as a "bosky oasis in the city." A second outlet opened its doors uptown, where Billy and Tom expanded into cut flowers. But it was only at their third and largest store that things took a new turn.

Today the address on lower Broadway would be smack in the middle of SoHo, but back then it was off the beaten track. It nevertheless became a destination shop, selling a bit of everything. Besides flowers, you could find antiques, materials, knickknacks. The mix of old and new, rustic and rusty, might seem quite run-of-the-mill today, but in its time it was unique.

"Remember, that was long before stores were selling grungy old stuff with peeling paint," Billy points out. "It was long before Martha Stewart. People didn't even put flowers in clear glass back then. It was all about modernism, Calvin Klein and capsule-shaped tables, leather, gray, black, and white. Meanwhile we were telling people to buy old painted furniture and use lots of color, color, color."

Jeffrey also remembers it as the first store in Manhattan to unabashedly sell the costless alongside the costly.

"Billy mixed the reverent with the irreverent," he says.

The most infamous marriage of extremes involved an errant car part. Walking along a lane behind the store one morning, Billy spied something battered lying on the rough surface of cobblestones. It turned out to be a muffler and tailpipe that had been driven over so many times by garbage trucks, which were practically the only vehicles using the narrow lane, that it had been flattened and had rusted into a beautiful shade of orange. He took it back to the store and, without doing anything to it, put it in a window display, right next to a piece of Lohmeier crystal.

"I used it in various displays over the years," Billy says. "People kept asking about that mushed muffler and wanted to buy it. It became my joke. People thought it was this amazing quote-unquote art item. Finally I sold it for three hundred dollars."

In the same way, Billy would take something old and used to create something new. He would put a lightbulb on an extension cord and run it into a discarded can, or he'd pick up something at the flea market and stick a flower in it. Often, it was those items that got noticed first.

"People would come into the store and say, 'Oh, my God, how much is that? It's fabulous.' And I'd tell them, 'It's not fabulous, it's garbage.'"

Billy's candor didn't end there, either. He would also recommend that instead of coming to him to buy things, his customers might go out and find the trash on their own. All they had to do was keep their eyes open, scour the sidewalks, and go with their instincts. But he didn't have an easy time persuading people to trust their own judgment.

"They would put something from the store on the counter, and say, 'What do you think? Should I get this?' And I'd say, 'Frankly, I don't care. Do *you* like it?' And they'd say, 'I do, but I don't know if it'll go with the other things I have.' I said, 'If you've got the money to buy it, and you like it, then buy it. If it ends up you don't like it, give it away. It's not a big deal.'"

The outcome of all this cross-counter banter was that Madderlake became a kind of ideas workshop. Customers, after being repeatedly confronted with the fact that they might have a taste for the unusual, for trash even, slowly began to reassess their concepts of taste. If someone was convinced that he had no taste at all, Billy tried to persuade him otherwise.

"Everyone has the ability to make an aesthetic decision," he says. "Most people don't believe that about themselves. I believe that if I really like a piece of glass that costs one dollar at a flea market and a goblet by Lohmeier that costs three hundred dollars, and I think they're both beautiful and I put them together, then that's appropriate. It's not that one is more valuable than the other, but that they look great together. But most people are terrified. They think, Oh, God, I've got it wrong—someone's going to say something."

Billy watched his customers, or his students, rather, gain self-confidence, experiment, and test their own preconceived notions. Someone who in the beginning couldn't do without his opinion would suddenly know exactly what they wanted. A good time to see this happen was on Sunday mornings. Billy would go to the Grand Street market and pick out something he liked—such as the glass sock darner—and then bring it back to the store, wash it, and put it on a shelf.

"Sometimes it would be some obscure thing, a very odd little item, and I'd mark it up royally because I knew it was a one-of-a-kind piece. A client would walk in, go straight to the new acquisition, and buy it."

These were small victories for Billy. He had taught someone to open their eyes to the possibilities every object offers, although by doing so he was, in effect, writing himself and Madderlake out of the equation. But he didn't mind.

"For me it wasn't about making a buck. I loved the fact that they appreciated my sensibility and my eye, but they had the eye too. They came into the shop and out of that huge space, they picked up that one thing I just bought."

Today Billy's philosophy on décor has become his business. Often asked to address groups and conferences, he says over a lectern what he used to say over a shop counter. He repeats the message he has advanced since the 1970s, except for one difference: Instead of Styrofoam, glass sock darners, and mushed mufflers, the focus now is floral.

"Flowers are a great way to show what I mean, because they're a temporary medium. People are afraid they're going to make mistakes with a flower arrangement. I tell them, 'Well, how bad a mistake can you make? The things are dead. If you pick beautiful things and put them together, how ugly can it be?'

"The idea sounds like New Age hoo-ha, but it's definitely never been said this way. It's not like some self-help mantra.

You learn from it. You learn how to alter what you're thinking about. It's just empowering people. It's perhaps forty percent flowers, but the rest is about self-confidence."

Some people might find the connection between flowers and garbage as hard to grasp as the one between a dishwasher rack and a work of art, but to Jeffrey the link is obvious.

"Billy has an eye for seeing the essential beauty of form and material, whatever it is. I'm just a copycat."

Copycat or not, Jeffrey needed to be in the right frame of mind to follow Billy's philosophy, and he needed to be in the right place at the right time. Allen Street was where all three coincided.

Jeffrey moved to Allen Street in the early 1990s. The three-story brownstone belonged to Amerigo Marras, a Sardinian who once owned the nearby Anarchy Bookstore, the sort of place that probably thrived three decades earlier. It was at the Anarchy, in the years before the Internet, that you could find books on topics like how to make a bomb at home.

"I don't think it would be allowed to exist today," says Jeffrey wryly.

Amerigo bought two adjacent houses, then immediately sold one of them. The house he kept was said to be among the oldest surviving dwellings in Manhattan, dating back to the 1820s. The neighborhood was the perfect place for an apartment built of scraps, seeing it stood almost at the heart of what had once been Ragpickers' Row.

"Ragpickers' Row is the most wretched haunt occupied by human beings in the New World," James Cabe wrote in his 1882 book *New York by Sunlight & Gaslight*. "It is easily found. You leave the Bowery at Bayard street, go down two blocks to Mulberry street, and it is just around the corner. Anybody can tell you where the ragpickers live. There is no mistaking the place. A junkman's cellar in the front of the house opens widely to the street, and, peering down, one may see a score of men and women half buried in dirty rags and paper, which they are gathering up and putting into bales for the paper mills. This is the general depot to which the ragpicker brings his odds and ends for sale after he has sorted them. Just as we emerge from this cellar a ragpicker, heavily laden, passes up the stoop and enters the hall above. Following him, we come to the small, badly-paved courtyard, which separates the front from the rear houses. Standing here and looking up, one beholds a sight that cannot be imagined. Rags to the right of him, rags to the left of him, on all sides nothing but rags. Lines in the yard draped with them, balconies festooned with them, fire-escapes decorated with them, windows hung with them, in short, every available object dressed in rags—and such rags! of every possible size, shape and color."

At 143 Allen Street, Amerigo took up residence on the top two floors and Jeffrey moved in below. Unlike many collectors, Jeffrey had never collected before moving to Allen Street and he wouldn't do it after he left. It was a phase in his life. Other phases have included being the head butler at the Waldorf Towers; a concierge at the Ritz-Carlton; a massage therapist; an assistant to, at various times, an upholsterer, an electrician, and a photographer who specialized in nineteenth-century techniques; a cater waiter; a furniture designer; a musician; and an actor in the movie *Someone to Watch Over Me*. He now works at Banana Republic.

"Collecting was the latest strategy in my life," he says. "There's no connection between my past and collecting. I have no career, no label. Wherever I found myself in life, I tried to be resourceful. I collected out of need and creativity. Nor was I an intentional collector. There were times, the way the streets looked, the time of day or night, especially night, or what I saw over on the other side of the [Christie Street] park, I knew I'm going to find something. And almost always I'd be right."

Over the next seven years, Allen Street was Jeffrey's work in progress, constantly being fixed up and touched up every time he found a new prop or a can of paint, or received a house present. The shell he began with made no sense at all, with its walls of badly installed sheetrock, ceilings that dropped in places for no reason, ugly floors, a conduit that stuck out prominently, and lots of construction lines that never had any resolution but just ended halfway across a room.

"Every time I acquired some new bonanza, I would start thinking where I could use it. My whole aim was to make things unintentional look intentional. I liked to see how things evolved—the interplay of what's available, what's necessary, what's possible, the ideas that emerge."

The dining room ceiling, with its starburst and triangular letters, took months to complete, and in the end became Jeffrey's pride and joy. He built the kitchen out of found cabinets, and a shower from found wood. Out of other found pieces he made a beveled frame for a rescued antique fan, which all went above the door into the bathroom. He put pebbles around the raised toilet, to give it a Japanese effect, and behind an old wall mirror he put a light in order to pick out the zigzag pattern of scratch marks. Every object, no matter how small or insignificant, had a history; and all that was missing were the plaques to explain which object was found or donated and which Dumpster or acquaintance it had come from.

"I tried to give things their just," says Jeffrey. "I tried to celebrate events that took place in my life and in that house, things that other people would say, 'This has to be corrected' or 'We use the clean side of that piece of wood.' I would often go for what wasn't obvious. Every vista was so saturated with things going on, and yet it wasn't cacophony. It was just mysterious."

Allen Street gained a reputation for being avant-garde and bohemian. This was as much because of the revolving-door policy, which meant the guest next to you at dinner could as easily be from off the street as from off the latest plane from France, as it was because of the warm browns and rich textures of the interior, which made you think you were in a chalet somewhere deep in Central Europe.

"It wasn't always an easy way of living," Jeffrey admits in retrospect, "because you usually landed up doing more than your share of work. But it was good. No one thought of it then, but they realize now that those were the best years of their lives. I felt at the time that they should realize it—that this was as good as it gets."

In the same year Barat made his movie, Amerigo put the house up for sale. The buyers were two well-known American artists. Even at the time of the sale—long before the last residents had moved out, the house was finally gutted, and his own seven-year-long work was destroyed—Jeffrey was struck by the fact that the demise of Allen Street, the eviction of its residents and the end of their lifestyle, was set in motion by, of all people, artists.

"I think it's deeply ironic that they would buy a house they knew was inhabited by people who couldn't afford to move, knowing everything, which they did," he says.

But the Lower East Side was changing, and even though Jeffrey could have gotten a respite of several months, he would have had to get out in the end. Moneyed people were moving into the neighborhood, chic restaurants were opening, and the tenement houses where ragpickers once crowded into single rooms were becoming prime real estate. Several years later, Iona and her fellow food collectors on Rivington Street, only a few blocks away, would be facing the same dilemma.

For weeks Jeffrey and his housemate, Sean, regularly put things out on the sidewalk, behind signs that read FOR FREE and MORE STUFF INSIDE. Many of the items that had originally been found or given to them were now being put back into circulation.

Amerigo had already left for Europe, where he'd bought an apartment in Nice that had once belonged to the writer Antoine de Saint-Exupéry. After several months, word reached Allen Street that his health had declined rapidly. Jeffrey, concerned that they had not parted on the best of terms after the sale, wrote to his former landlord and friend, and after some time passed he got a call back. During the conversation, Amerigo said something that echoed a sentiment Jeffrey had expressed many times before then.

"He said that the years in Allen Street were the good times, the best times. He told me that selling the house was the gravest mistake he ever made. We were his family. We had Thanksgiving together. We watched over him. We took care of each other. He didn't realize how good he had it. This web of relationships that he loved to rail against was also what kept him a healthy, happy man."

This same kind of camaraderie, it seemed, was what kept Iona, Flo, and Channing balanced. They were together, they were collecting, and they were happy. But Amerigo had given all that up when he left Allen Street, and a few months later he had a stroke and died.

When Jeffrey was thrown out of the Lower East Side, he left not only his residence but also his prime focus. Needing to escape from New York for a while, he went to the place that's always replenished him, Paris. Late one night shortly after he arrived, he got an urgent call from New York. It was Sean. A truck loaded with numerous articles from Allen Street that they had chosen to keep had been stolen while it was parked somewhere overnight. Most of the things listed in (1) through (26), including the skinhead Last Supper, the meat scale, and the mantelpiece, were lost forever.

Difficult though it was, Jeffrey maintained an interest in Allen Street. It had been his passion for seven years, and he wanted to see what happened to it. He had coffee several times with the new owners' daughter, although she never showed him what was being done inside the building.

"I told her, 'It's okay. This is your house now to do with what you want. I enjoyed it while I had it.'"

After a while, she stopped returning his calls and Jeffrey found himself visiting the Bowery less often. Many months later, though, he started collaborating with a musician who lived around the corner from Allen Street, so he found himself visiting his old stomping ground almost daily. The construction at the house was still going on, two years later, and outside the front door there were always several Dumpsters full of the scraps of the scraps that he'd once used.

"I knew they had gutted the place. What I didn't realize

was that they'd torn the whole rear off, which I built totally out of code."

When Jeffrey saw bits and pieces of that large back room in the Dumpster, he was curious to find out what the demolition people had thought of his nonexistent building skills. Using that as an excuse, he phoned the owners' daughter again. She told him that the men who'd dismantled the room had been very impressed with his ingenuity, although they had no idea it was the first room Jeffrey had ever built or that he had done it with scraps from the street. At one point, Jeffrey said he would love to take pictures of Allen Street in its new transformed shape, with everything gone.

"Suddenly the whole tone changed," he says, "and she became extremely defensive and guarded. She said, 'I wouldn't feel comfortable about that. This isn't your story anymore.'"

chapter 6

the dealer

Waiting outside the Frick Museum at three one morning, or
what Steven Dixon calls the netherworld hour, I can see why
collectors love being out at this time. The streets are empty,
you can go through garbage without anyone staring at you,
be it a surly doorman or a disgusted passerby, and the city is
uncharacteristically quiet until dawn, when you're met by a
cacophony not of car engines and horns but of birdcalls.

The netherworld stillness this morning, however, is suddenly
broken by someone walking through an opening in the wall
of Central Park, then crossing Fifth Avenue. It's Steven. With
his oversized white shirt hanging loosely around his pants, he
looks like he's just gotten out of bed. But his gait couldn't be
more lively, and he's pushing an empty four-wheel trolley, the
kind an old lady might fill with groceries. Without the trolley,
he would be swinging his arms in front of him like a marathon
walker: strong, purposeful.

Steven walks across Central Park only on the days of the
week that he collects on the Upper East Side. People aren't
allowed to be in the park at this hour, but Steven says he can
be. In the same confident way that Dave asserts he can tres-
pass onto a particular dump site, Steven claims he's one of
the few people the police don't bother in Central Park after
hours.

It wasn't always that way. When Steven first started collecting books, and he was still putting them in bags instead of in a trolley, the police would sometimes stop him. One night when he was walking a bit too fast down Fifth Avenue, bags in one hand, a recently found copy of Shakespeare in the other, the police thought he looked suspicious and wrestled him to the ground. His first words to them are typical of Steven, forthright and a bit facetious.

"How many burglars," he asked, "do you see running around with a copy of Shakespeare?"

Steven's route this particular morning falls within a four-square-mile grid. He will begin at the Frick, go east as far as East End Avenue, up a block, then west back to Fifth Avenue, and in this zigzagging motion he will gradually make his way northward. The buildings he goes to along the way fall into four categories: those he doesn't care about, seeing as they have never, in all his years of collecting, provided him with anything memorable; those he has already visited in the past twelve hours, because they put out their garbage from midday the previous day; those he still needs to visit; and those he has already visited but goes back to a second time, because they have a tendency to add more garbage in dribs and drabs throughout the night.

On arriving at a pile, Steven can immediately tell whether something has been added or taken away, or if someone else has been there before him. He circles the garbage like a tracker in the jungle might do the leftover carcass of an animal.

"A black-bag guy has been here," he will say. "See how the bags are torn."

When he reaches something that interests him, Steven moves quickly. He doesn't go for everything, only boxes, stacks of paper tied up in string, and transparent recycling bags. With a box, he will first look at its size and condition. The older, smaller, and more discolored it is, the better. Those features suggest to him that someone found it in a cupboard and threw it out without properly inspecting the contents. Inside might only be a few books, but quite possibly one of them will be that rarity that's worth five hundred other books. He hits the box with the palm of his hand or kicks it softly, to hear what sound it makes.

"If it's heavy, newspaper. If it's hollow, books."

Should the sound be right, he lifts up the box, turns it on its side, nimbly slices it from corner to corner with a blade, and then pries open the perforation he's made to see what's inside. If it's a tied-up bundle that catches his eye, he cuts the string, takes what he wants, then reties it.

To anyone passing by a few moments later, Steven might never have been there at all. The stacks are always replaced, and the slit made by his blade is hardly noticeable. Like the Dumpster divers, he is almost painstakingly fastidious in the way he likes to leave garbage exactly as he found it. And he expects nothing less from other collectors. When we come across bags in disarray, their contents lying scattered all over the place, he mutters something about the black-bag people being "terrorists," their tactics "slash-and-burn." That doesn't mean he dislikes them—in fact, he admires them and sometimes even listens to their suggestions on where to find books—but their methods don't make life any easier for him.

"Try to tell a doorman that you're not the one responsible for the mess," he says, then steers his trolley to a bunch of bags and boxes just west of Madison Avenue and stops. "This is a good building."

Ignoring the obvious things closest to us, he zeroes in on something behind them, a heap of catalogs from Sotheby's and Christie's. It's as if he knew they were there all along. Without looking at the bundles, he takes them by the string and thoughtlessly tosses them into his trolley.

"I always get something for these," he says. "Fifty bucks for the best, maybe a hundred. A Marilyn Monroe auction, the Duke and Duchess of Windsor, Jackie O, Princess Di— those are the good ones." A few days earlier he had picked up a Marilyn Monroe catalog and sold it almost immediately for sixty dollars. "Now that's good garbage."

He sells the catalogs, which have become almost as important a part of Steven's business as books, on eBay, as well as copies of the theater magazine *Playbill*. The most he has gotten for a *Playbill*, a Barbra Streisand one-night-only concert, was fifty dollars.

"The funny thing about *Playbill*s is that you never find one or two. You always find them by the hundreds."

One place where it's particularly profitable to find them by the hundreds is at the annual Tony Awards, because each one can fetch as much as thirty dollars. "It's easy money," Steven says, but then adds something that reminds me he is disclosing yet another piece of his treasure map, "if you *know* it's easy money." When the show came around this year, he prepared to stand outside the theater with his trolley and take in as many castoff programs as he could. But then it rained—and nothing terminates the routine of a collector of paper like rain does, not even snow—so he skipped the event.

For most *Playbill*s Steven asks a standard price (four dollars for the better-known shows), although he'll ask a lot more should he come up with a good enough reason. After overhearing a woman in a thirft store tell her friend that she was a Ralph Fiennes fan and had just spent seventy-five dollars on a *Playbill* for a show he'd done five years earlier, Steven rushed home and pushed up every Ralph Fiennes *Playbill* he had to twenty dollars. When Katharine Hepburn died, Steven jammed eBay with everything he had about her, *Playbill*s, books, anything.

"In the eBay world, when someone famous dies, suddenly everyone wants something about that person. At the end of two weeks, that's it. People don't care anymore. Then I take it off."

Auction catalogs and *Playbill*s are the only nonbook items that Steven collects, even though he is regularly tempted to make an exception. Later that morning, just as a garbage truck is closing in on us, we come across a box of old *Life* magazines. They are all obviously part of a collection, put together some time ago by someone who was fascinated by the first landing on the moon, the assassination of John F. Kennedy, and Watergate. Steven estimates they could fetch twenty dollars apiece, but he passes them up. He spends a few minutes browsing through them (he always makes time to browse), but he finally drops them back into their boxes.

"I don't bother with magazines anymore. I had to make a choice. I decided books, and only books."

When Steven was laid off from Chase Bank in the mid-1990s, he started selling secondhand books on the street near Washington Square. Reading had been a passion of his from an early age. He read better than other kids, and he went for the less conventional. He remembers devouring Cornelius Ryan's seven-hundred-page history of the airborne invasion of

Europe, *A Bridge Too Far*, when he was eight. But reading for pleasure and selling books for a living, as he discovered on Washington Square, were two very different things. Being a dealer had few advantages.

"I wasn't into the people who came by," he recalls. "You wait on their every breath. Will she take it? Yes . . . no . . . yes . . . no. They always complained about the prices. 'Why is this book five dollars?' they'd say. 'I'll give you two dollars.' Would they do that in a bookstore?"

His colleagues were unwelcoming. The man at the next table, if he wasn't in a bad mood, told Steven he would never sell anything and suggested he pack up and leave.

"I thought to myself, I don't want to turn out like him."

On his way home one afternoon, Steven found some books on a sidewalk in the West Village. He took several and put them on his table the next day. He started acquiring more and more of his books this way, instead of from secondhand stores, until he realized that the time he was spending trying to sell books could be spent finding books to sell.

It wasn't hard choosing which line of work to give up. He closed his stand on Washington Square and started building up his book business by trolling the streets for books he could sell to other dealers. He learned from trial and error, and if he had to list the guidelines he follows today, they would probably go something like this.

Rule 1. Good Books Can Turn Up Where You Least Expect Them

Steven almost always remembers exactly where he found a book, especially if it was a good one. The date might be fuzzy, and he won't recall the building's number, but he can give you the avenues and the cross streets without a second's hesitation.

It was on West Sixty-sixth Street, for instance, that he saw a pile of newspapers early one morning. It looked like any other pile of newspapers, until he noticed a single book jammed in at the very top, as if it had been stuffed in as an afterthought. Steven was able to pull out the book without even cutting the string that bound them together.

When he checked the name on the spine, his heart jumped. It was volume 1 of Henry Stanley's *In Darkest Africa*. The edition was obviously very old, but he didn't know it was a first edition until he opened it. That's also when he saw that it had been signed by Stanley himself.

Like any collector who has made a great find, Steven wanted to share his excitement. He called over to the doorman of the apartment building the garbage belonged to.

"This is a valuable book," he said, holding it in the air.

The doorman pulled a face. He was unimpressed. "Just make sure that you tie up those papers before you leave," he said impatiently, then went back into the building.

For several weeks after that, Steven returned to the building in the hope of finding volume 2, but nothing ever turned up.

Rule 2. Be Happy with Whatever You Get

Steven sold volume 1 of *In Darkest Africa* to a dealer for three hundred dollars. A week later, he returned to the store and saw the book prominently displayed in the rare-books section. Selling price: seventeen hundred dollars.

If Steven knew back then what he knows today (he found the Stanley volume early in his collecting career), he probably could have negotiated a better price than three hundred dollars—but not much better. For no matter how knowledgeable he has become or how familiar he is with book prices, he knows that he can't ask the same as a dealer. The inequity annoys him.

"If I had a shop, and I put the book in a window, and I just sat there in a rocking chair, someone would see it and say, 'Ooh, ooh, I'll take that.' If I took the same book and put it on a table, like I did in Washington Square, they'd say, 'I'll give you twenty bucks.'"

What's worse, some dealers also want to know the provenance of Steven's merchandise. If he tells the truth, that he found it on the sidewalk, then they either don't want it or they use its origin as an excuse to offer him less than they would someone who has a story they find more acceptable.

When I ask Steven why he doesn't just concoct a background for the books he finds (in the way, say, Dave conjures whole histories for his sets of false teeth), if only to make the dealer happy and to get himself a better price, he frowns.

"It's too hard. I just take my chances."

If anything has helped change this imbalance, it's the Internet. Now there is a much vaster market for Steven's books and Dave's jewelry, for any collector's mongo, in fact, a place where clients never ask who you are or how you got your merchandise. The staff at a rare-book store like Ursus in the Hotel Carlyle, one of the top dealers in the country, might look at Steven suspiciously when he comes to their door, but that never happens online.

"In a store I have to work through all these layers. They look at me, then at the book, and then they try decide if I stole it. On the Internet, it's one person dealing with another."

As a result, Steven has developed what he calls "a virtual dealership" and "eBay relationships." He does regular electronic business with galleries and merchants in England, who contact him for catalogs. He doesn't tell them where his stock comes from, the recipients don't ask, and everyone gets what they want.

Rule 3. People Who Don't Collect Books Don't Know Books

Lots of people tell Steven where to find books. For example, a black-bag guy might say, "I saw some books up on Eighty-fifth Street. Get up there quick! Before the sanitation truck comes."

In the beginning, Steven used to rush off, only to reach the recommended spot and find books that he would never consider, such as *Reader's Digest* condensed versions and school textbooks. As a result of the detour, his whole schedule for the morning would have been ruined.

"Now I never get excited when people tell me about free books," he says, "because most of the time what's a good book to them is very plain to me."

Rule 4. Time Spent Looking for the Right Buyer Could Be Time Spent Looking for Books

Steven occasionally makes an exception to his rule about collecting books and only books. Once, he found a box of late-nineteenth-century German erotica, or as he better describes it, "photographs of a bunch of overaged men running around naked with a bunch of overweight women."

He had never sold photographs before, let alone erotica, and he didn't know who specialized in it. He wasted several days trying to find out, but he got nowhere. In the end, he sold the whole batch to a porn store near Times Square. He needed eBay, but he hadn't started using it yet.

Rule 5. Time Spent Looking for the Right Buyer Could be Worth a Lot of Money

Steven knows he took a loss on the erotica, but that's nothing compared to what happened with another nonbook collection he found.

Normally Steven doesn't bother with Dumpsters, but several years ago he was drawn to one off Central Park West because there was a book tossed on the very top. It turned out to be a copy of Madame Chiang Kai-shek's *Sure Victory*, inscribed by her in English and Chinese to a man named John Golden.

The Dumpster contained numerous other possessions of Golden's, whose apartment was being renovated. Over the next few weeks, Steven purposely made regular detours past the address, to see what else had been thrown out. At the same time, he was able to piece together the life of the man whom the castoffs had once belonged to.

Golden, he learned, had been a Broadway producer of dozens of plays, and a Broadway theater still carries his name. He died in 1955, but for some reason his effects were only being thrown out almost five decades later. Among them Steven found several good books, but a more valuable discovery was Golden's old theater contracts, about one hundred of them, signed by actors like Edward G. Robinson.

"The Robinson signature alone was worth five hundred dollars," Steven says, a fact he unfortunately didn't know at the time.

Along with the contracts, he found a manila envelope, inside of which was a notebook with a list of other famous people whose signatures Golden had collected, as well as some of the items they had signed. These included a card signed by Benjamin Disraeli and a letter signed by Aaron Burr.

As with the erotic photographs of the overweight nudists romping through the Black Forest, in those pre-eBay days, Steven once again had a product he wasn't familiar with and had never traded before. He knew that the signatures would be worth a lot to the right person, but who was that person and how did he find him? He went to various dealers, but they all wanted to know the same thing: How had he come upon a letter signed by Aaron Burr?

"I had heard of an antiques dealer on the radio," Steven says, and mentions the shop's name. "They said, 'We deal in signatures.' So I went there. The guy took a quick look at what I brought in—there was a lot of stuff—and he said he'd give me a thousand bucks. Just like that. And I took it."

Not long after that, Steven was watching an episode of *Antiques Roadshow* that included a valuation of some old signatures. It didn't take him long to realize that what he'd had in the Golden collection was a lot better, and worth a lot more than he'd gotten.

"The dealer probably sold those signatures for a gazoodle of money."

Rule 6. Remember, It's Only Garbage

Whenever Steven talks about what happened with the Stanley volume and the Golden collection—and a couple of other instances like these—there isn't any bitterness in his voice.

"Everyone's happy," he says. "I got money, the dealer got money, and the buyer gets what he wants." In the case of the signatures, he admits he got screwed, but he was a thousand dollars richer than he'd been that morning. "And if I hadn't found them, they'd be landfill somewhere."

Rule 7. It's Okay to Be Disappointed

This rule doesn't come up often, given that Steven believes so firmly in Rule 6, but it did the morning he found a first edition of James Joyce's *Ulysses*.

A building where he'd never found books had put out several boxes, and inside one was an old paperback with a blue cover. After Steven saw the title and the author, he looked inside to check where and when it had been published: Paris. 1922.

Once he had those two pieces of information, he knew that it was a first edition and was worth a lot of money. But when he turned it over, his heart sank. The back cover was torn.

"It was worth nothing," he says. "That was a very sad moment."

His next James Joyce discovery would have a happier ending. Not only was the copy in perfect condition, but it wasn't on its own. A first edition of *Finnegans Wake* was lying right next to a first edition of Thomas Wolfe's *You Can't Go Home Again*. He got five hundred dollars for the two.

Rule 8. Never Get too Attached to a Book or, for That Matter, to Anything

An old man whom Steven was vaguely acquainted with owned an apartment block in the East Eighties that he lived in all by himself. All of the apartments, instead of being occupied by tenants, were full of books, making the building, in effect, a book warehouse.

"He hung on to everything," Steven says. "He must have had at least a hundred thousand books. There was even a rare-book room, where he kept signed first editions."

The old man had a sweetheart deal with an auction house that allowed him to take all the books that were acquired from the estates it was handling, sell what he could, and then split the profits. It seldom worked that way, and even though there were titles the old man was said to have sold for as much as twenty thousand dollars apiece—truth or urban legend?—he kept all the money.

His behavior didn't endear him to many people, and it only got worse. When he finally sold his apartment building, he was given time to clear out the books, but he didn't. Even at that stage he refused to give away a single copy, not even to people he knew. Eventually the books were taken away, apartment by apartment, or placed on the sidewalk. The old man moved to an assisted-living home, where he died a year later.

"I realized then," Steven says, "that the whole thing about owning stuff forever is really silly. Because you never do."

Steven keeps as few books as possible in his home, and he collects only what he is confident he will sell that very same day. His aim is to be able to head home at midday with an empty trolley, everything found during the morning now gone. And even though he reads books avidly—about a title a week— he never keeps them.

Rule 9. Most People Think That if You Collect off the Sidewalk, You're a Bum

Steven has crossed paths with numerous celebrities. Some encounters go off better than others. George Plimpton, whom Steven liked, told him that he had lots of books but he never gave them away. The artist Damien Hirst (of formaldehyde-cow fame) told him that he used to collect off the streets of London.

The meetings with well-known actors have been less auspicious. Woody Allen hasn't once returned Steven's early-morning greetings ("He's very serious. I say, 'Hi Woody,' and he puts his head down"). John Travolta chased him away from outside a Scientology building on the Upper East Side, although Steven suspects that was because the actor thought he was studying the garbage for incriminating evidence about the sect. And even though Sigourney Weaver probably didn't mean to offend Steven, she did.

"She came up to me and said, 'I just love what you people do, recycling.'" Steven repeats the words, "'You people'?!"

The one thing that Steven hates more than anything else is the way all sidewalk collectors get lumped together. The spokesman at the sanitation department does it because of policy, but most people do it because they don't know any better. Steven often gets mistaken for a canner, and if it's not money he gets offered, it's pity, stares and, worst of all, disdain.

Most collectors ignore this, but Steven can't. He has carved a very important niche for himself, but because it is within the realm of garbage, it is somehow seen as unremarkable, if it is seen at all. He works more diligently than anyone in an office, seven days a week, rising when it's still dark, working till noon, resting for a few hours, and then going out again, making sure he's in bed early so he can get a good night's sleep in order to be fresh the next morning. Is that someone who should be regarded as a bum?

But recognition eludes him, even in those rare moments when someone actually sees him triumph. A chauffeur parked on a side street early one morning witnessed Steven find a book that he'd been after for a long time, *James Bond's Guide to the Birds of Jamaica*. It was a first edition from the 1920s and was written by a friend of Ian Fleming, who would one day use the birder's name for the fictional agent 007. All of this meant nothing to the chauffeur.

"I was so excited, but this guy just didn't get it. I told him that the book was worth about three hundred dollars. He said, 'Yeah, right.' He didn't believe me. When someone finds a gold necklace, everyone says, 'Wow!' even though it might be gold-plated and worthless. But if you find a book, how do you explain to someone who doesn't know that a book has value?"

Rule 10. Garbage Isn't in the Eye of the Beholder but in the Way You Arrange it

Steven was finishing off his rounds one day, just after seven A.M., when he saw a huge pile of art books tied up outside a building. He knew from experience that the building's super-intendent was accustomed to putting out garbage the previous night, which meant that the books had probably been there for at least twelve hours. Yet it was clear from their condition that no one had paid them any attention. Steven could have understood this if the books were on a street that few people reached, but they lay on a busy pedestrian thorough-fare, less than half a block from a subway station.

As he always does before he selects the books he wants, he arranged them side by side, turning the sidewalk into a tempo-rary bookshelf. No sooner had he done this than a man in a suit walked up and started browsing through them. Steven ignored him.

"I'm used to people doing that," he says. "People who wouldn't bother to look at a pile of books tied up with string will all of a sudden stop when the books are neatly arranged in a row on the sidewalk. I transform garbage."

It was only when the man started walking away with a book in his hand that Steven reacted.

"I said, 'Hey, where are you going with that?' He said, 'Oh, you want this?' I was so angry."

The man grudgingly asked Steven how much he wanted for it, so he said ten dollars. The man paid him and then handed over his business card.

"He was a rare-book collector. If I'd known that, I wouldn't have sold it to him."

Steven maintains his brisk pace as he heads down Park Avenue, not stopping at every accretion of bags and boxes but only at the ones that draw his attention. I recall the words of another collector about good collecting being a combination of luck and intuition. Steven seems to have plenty of both. He likes to compare himself to the Walter Huston character in *The Treasure of the Sierra Madre*.

"He knew where the gold was, and I know where the books are," he says. "I just have to look at the neighborhood. I can tell from the height of the windows if there is stuff." Steven always accentuates the word *stuff*, loading it with possibilities. "The bigger the windows, the higher the ceilings, the better the stuff. Even if there are no bookcases, they'll have coffee tables with books on them. I know that I'll make a hundred dollars walking up and down a street."

Steven sometimes points out buildings like a tour guide and refers to them by the name of an author whose work he found there, especially if it was valuable. At the Saul Bellow Building he got some first editions by the Nobel Prize–winner, but the Ian Fleming Building was even better. Steven pulled out of a clear plastic bag three first-edition James Bond novels, all in good condition. *Dr. No* and *From Russia, with Love* brought him several hundred dollars each, while *Casino Royale,* the very first Bond novel, he sold for a thousand dollars.

"For the British edition, you get over ten thousand," he says, as if in preparation for the day he might stumble across it. But this morning, as we pass the Ian Fleming Building, there's nothing.

Whenever Steven picks up a book, it doesn't take him long to decide whether it's desirable or not. He holds it as if he's weighing it, then opens it and takes a cursory look at the date of publication and the dust jacket. Dust jackets are imperative, and he rejects anything without one. If there happens to be a good dust jacket all on its own, he takes that too, just in case he might be able to use it in the future on an edition whose dust jacket is missing or damaged.

He is as strict about the books he puts into his trolley as he is about the daily route he follows. He doesn't take computer books, medical books, or legal books. He avoids many British authors and most modern novels. He passes up Jeffrey Archer and Pat Conroy but takes Toni Morrison. "She doesn't write as much, so she's worth more." He knows he'll get only a dollar each for the others, and, as he puts it, "That's just above cans."

Steven's motivation is purely financial, and his choices of what books to take often go against his better literary judgement. Consider the apartment building where he finds, among other things, *The Language of Letting Go* by Melody Beatty and *The Kennedys* by Theodore Sorensen. He takes the one he would like to leave, and he leaves the one he'd like to take.

"I hate these self-help books," he says about *Letting Go,* "but people are caught up in them now. Self-help and how to have a baby. You wonder how people had babies before these books came out." Still, he drops it in his trolley. As for the Sorensen, he knows he won't be able to sell it. "There are so many millions of books that the bookstores don't want, *millions* of them."

Those books, ironically, are usually what Steven himself likes to read, which is history, books about the origin of the Bible, and parapsychology. The sidewalk has also introduced him to the writings of Michio Kaku, a professor of theoretical physics, and Isaac Asimov, and he has just finished a book on exorcism by the Jesuit priest Malachi Martin. When I ask him what he recommends I read, he doesn't hesitate before answering Barbara Tuchman's *March to Folly* and *A People's History of the United States* by Howard Zinn.

Steven looks at his watch after the Ian Fleming Building and, noticing the time, he starts walking even faster. He is behind schedule. In much the same way that he remembers where he has made certain discoveries, he knows when he needs to be at a particular building.

"I've got it timed," he says. "I know my route, the buildings I have to go to, and the exact time I need to be there."

He also knows, after six years of collecting, what to expect when he arrives. If Steven had a score sheet for the east and west sides of Central Park, it would probably look something like this: paperback versus hardback, more trivial book versus more scholarly, a biography of Jack Kerouac versus *The Autobiography of William O. Douglas,* good fiction versus bad.

"The income level is much higher on the Upper East Side, but the level of books the people read is much lower. I'll find very good art books and really lousy hardcover novels. Danielle Steel, Judith Krantz."

Another difference he's noticed is that the residents east of Central Park donate books to thrift stores, while Upper West Siders don't. Why Steven knows this is because he not only collects books, he also buys them. Once he has finished collecting for the day, he scouts out the thrift stores. He will also peruse telephone poles for any For Sale signs, especially the ones that *don't* advertise books.

"You're more likely to find a bargain in the home of someone who doesn't put any value in books." A few days earlier he had picked up thirty great books for thirty dollars. "The woman was more interested in what she got for the TV." He says, "I can go into a book sale and spend a hundred dollars, go somewhere else and sell those same books for two hundred. I double my money just like that."

Books and everything else in thrift stores aren't mongo, but they probably would have been if not for an act of charity. Which is why collectors like going there. And their time collecting on the sidewalk has also taught them how to use their money judiciously when they do actually buy something.

"If I found Ian Fleming on the sidewalk and sold it for a thousand dollars," Steven says, "I can't see myself paying twenty dollars for a book in a thrift store that I might be able to sell for a hundred."

Thrift stores are often the recipient of items that the giver doesn't know the value of, and the chance of a collector finding a bargain there is entirely dependent on whether the staff knows. The shop that Steven went into one day didn't know the value of a first edition of Tom Clancy's *The Hunt for Red October,* so he bought it for one dollar in the morning and then sold it later that day for two hundred dollars.

"If you saw the book, you wouldn't know it was a first

edition—no publisher, the print looks like it was done on a typewriter, and it weighs two pounds."

He has, since then, found two more first editions of *Red October* at thrift stores and then sold them for a sizable profit. Each discovery, besides making him very happy, has also made him wonder how a book about a Russian submarine could be worth such a lot of money. Who decided? How did they decide? And how did they settle on a particular figure? The answer he's come up with is worthy not of a Tom Clancy novel but maybe a John Grisham one. You could call it *The Syndicate*. Steven does.

Whenever Steven has to find out the price he should be asking for a book, he heads to the nearest Barnes & Noble and consults the most recent book-pricing guides. What he repeatedly discovers, though, is that the figures that he would give certain first editions don't come anywhere close to what the book-pricing guides give. You can get one thousand dollars for *Red October* and thirty-five thousand dollars for a signed *Harry Potter and the Sorcerer's Stone*, but only fifty dollars for Sloan Wilson's *The Man in the Gray Flannel Suit* or *Portnoy's Complaint* by Philip Roth. To Steven it sounds suspiciously like the work of a syndicate, a group of people who give values to books not because of what they're worth but because certain people, namely themselves, own copies.

"A book by a vacuum cleaner salesman is worth more than a classic of American literature?" he asks. "It's like the Dow Jones getting together and deciding what share prices should be."

Steven knows better than to condemn the pricing system, for it's precisely because of it that he stays in business. In much the same way, he profits off other people's ignorance, whims, oversights, and craziness, whether it's thrift stores that have no idea of what they've got on their shelves, decorators who throw out beautiful art books with the old wallpaper, the millionaire who paid more than one hundred dollars for a catalog of rock memorabilia after The Who's John Entwhistle died when he could've gotten it new from Sotheby's for twenty dollars, or the Argosy, a secondhand-book dealer on Fifty-ninth Street, where he can pay five dollars for a copy of, say, Ray Bradbury's *The Illustrated Man* one morning then sell it back to them later the same day for forty dollars.

Steven has come to accept these curiosities as part of his average workday, but he remains fascinated by the enigmatic reason for their existence: value. What is value? For Billy Jarecki, it is something you impose. Value is a personal judgment and has little to do with the object's origin. But for Steven it isn't as simple as walking into a flea market and falling in love with something or picking up a mushed muffler. Value can be imposed by The Syndicate, and it can change because a famous actor just died.

Steven can understand how he himself gives books value or, as he says half seriously, "turns water into wine," whether it's by taking them out of a bag or arranging them on the sidewalk. But three thousand for a first edition of Patricia Cornwell's *Postmortem*? How do you justify that? The Syndicate might ascribe the values to auctions or rarity, but Steven's answer is to call them "fake values." They are there not for him to understand, but that doesn't stop him from exploiting them. It's also quite likely that if he wasn't in this game, he would never believe that book collectors are prepared to pay the fake-value prices. But then again, as Steven repeatedly points out, he is a very different animal from a book collector.

"Collecting means you diligently go out in search of a specific thing to add to a collection. I find stuff to add to other people's collections. That makes me a finder."

At about five-thirty A.M. Steven's pace slows down for the first time, and the bounce leaves his step. The reason is a hostile doorman at a particularly large apartment building on Park Avenue. Doormen, for Steven, fall into three groups: those who want money or a favor in exchange for their books; those who don't want money but keep books for him anyway; and those who try to make life miserable for him and every other collector on the face of the earth.

"I have doormen friends and doormen enemies," he says, echoing the sentiments of most collectors.

Steven's nemesis, the doorman on Park Avenue, goes out of his way to be nasty. He repeatedly confronts him, accusing him of tearing apart garbage bags, which, as anyone who has ever watched him work can attest, is quite impossible. The fact that Steven encourages other collectors to clean up after themselves only makes the accusation more far-fetched.

"There's a certain degree of violence that goes with this job," Steven says. "And meanness."

The staff at certain buildings will purposely damage any garbage that might attract a collector, cutting the cords on TVs, running a razor through a sofa, or dousing books with water. They will put out dressers without drawers and chairs without cushions, deliberately rendering them unusable and undesirable.

"That's just spiteful," Steven says, and I realize then that it is these people, and not the sanitation department, who for collectors are the real Enemy Number 1.

"I saw a guy hosing down a pile of books one morning. I got so angry that I went straight over and picked them all up and put them in my trolley. I knew I wouldn't be able to sell them, but I wanted to prove a point. Then I went around the corner and dumped them."

That was a rare occasion for Steven, as he seldom gives himself the chance to dump books, taking today only what he knows he can sell today. But sometimes he doesn't have a choice, like the morning he met Ivana Trump. Just as he was finishing his rounds, she came out of a nearby brownstone. She was heading for her chauffeur-driven car, when she saw Steven and called him over. He mimics her accent.

"'Do you vahnt some books?' she asked me. 'I heff books.' She went back into the house, and I was expecting all these wonderful books. She came out with this huge bag full of paperback copies of her biography." He grunts. "That's not a book! I said thank you, took them around the corner, and put them in the trash."

We leave Park Avenue, turn west and then go north on Lexington Avenue. Steven will come back to this same spot in an hour's time, because there's a building here, a good building in his terms, that puts out garbage right before the sanitation truck arrives. The doorman's strategy might deter other collectors, but not him. He will be there promptly at seven A.M.

Steven has quickened his step again, the Park Avenue doorman a bad memory. Watching his businesslike attitude toward collecting, the professional way he crams every hour of his working day, zipping from one building to another so that he can meet his schedule and his personal quota, I can't see it ever getting tedious. But he assures me that before long it does.

"It's worst in winter," he says. "You have to remind your-self that there's a world out there."

I remember what Mr. Murphy said about how too much time on the street can make you imbalanced, and what Steven says suggests that the biggest contributing factor could be soli-tude. Which is why he does everything he can to stay in touch with other people while he's working.

He listens to talk radio. He talks to other collectors. He stays forever curious, watching people who walk by, reading papers that get thrown out, and then afterward developing his own thoughts on everything from the social fabric of New York to current events. For anyone who has the privilege of walking around with him, what he has to say is entertaining and often very funny. It could be about foreign nannies ("Most kids on the Upper East Side are going to grow up having Jamaican accents"), or the presidential envoy to Iraq, L. Paul Bremer III ("What do his friends call him? 'Hey, El Paul'"), or, of course, doormen ("One day they were suddenly *all* Eastern European, as if by magic, and they all knew each other" or "They are like special agents. They'll take a bullet for their building. 'Get away! That's my garbage!'").

More recently he has started doing what he describes as research but which is more like a game, where he tries to match the books on the *New York Times* bestseller list with the ones in the garbage. Because it doesn't take long for a book to go from first appearing on a bookstore shelf to being thrown away—Steven has seen it happen in as little as a week—he often sees a correlation. The diet books of Dr. Atkins are a case in point. Lots get sold, lots get discarded.

Some titles disprove his theory, and he isn't sure why. More recently there has been Hillary Clinton's *Living History* and

Ann Coulter's *Treason*, one of which was supposed to have sold over a million copies, while the other was constantly promoted on the radio stations he listens to. By Steven's calculation, he should have already seen at least one copy of each on the street, but he hasn't seen any.

"Either they [readers] love her and hold on to her, or the publisher is fudging the numbers," he says about Clinton. As for Coulter, a conservative Steven believes very few people really know about, he just guesses a reason. "I think some rich guy bought thousands and gave them to his friends."

The people who keep Steven most entertained when he's walking about, however, don't even do it consciously. They do it through their garbage. When he spots several boxes of papers on Eightieth Street, containing thousands of loose white sheets, he flips through them casually, as if he's suddenly got no schedule to follow. The pages he pulls out to read are excerpts from an interview given by Hubert Vedrine, the French foreign minister.

"I like to know what's going on in these buildings," he says. "You think it's just people living here, but it's a lot of other stuff going on."

While Steven greets other collectors, exchanges a few words with them, and even calls them his colleagues, the people he knows best from the sidewalk are the ones he has never actually met. Like John Golden, the theater producer. Like the man who was married to a Vanderbilt and collected photos about the Kennedy assassination and books about the military, several hundred of which got tossed when he moved. Like the devout Catholic who had been a football star at Notre Dame but liked male pornography, which was hidden away under his sport and religious memorabilia.

"The doorman had worked in the building twenty years.

When he saw the porn, he couldn't believe it. I knew more about this man by looking through his garbage than he did. By looking at someone's garbage you are almost able to go inside a building and look around their house. You find out about people. That's why it is more interesting to find books than to sell them."

Sometimes those books even *become* their owners, at least in Steven's eyes. He will say something like, "I was wandering around the Upper East Side when I found a guy named Jack Howard," and it sounds like the man was actually lying on the sidewalk when Steven stumbled over him.

Howard, a former chairman of the Scripps Howard media empire, collected ephemera, thirty bags of which were thrown out when he died in 1998. On going through the bags, Steven learned that Howard had been friends with every Republican president since Eisenhower. He found signed letters from them and photographs with them standing at Howard's side. Howard also tried to get his wife involved in movies—"just like Hearst," Steven adds, as if he has detected some strange media-mogul fascination with having a Hollywood wife—and there were lots of old movie scripts she had written in the 1930s.

Besides the scripts and the presidential memorabilia, Steven took numerous letters written to Howard and his wife by their daughter. They weren't worth anything, and they are among the few things that he admits keeping.

"I found them fascinating to read. She went on these trips to Europe, and there were lots of telegrams from ships, basically her itinerary—'We're going to this place, we're going to visit cousin so-and-so'—and I thought, isn't it sad that this person's life is on the sidewalk, totally meaningless."

*   *   *

Steven hits pay dirt outside a brownstone at about six-fifteen A.M. He finds several piles of art books, which he immediately starts arranging in his customary way, as if the pavement was his library.

The biggest volumes, the photographic books, come first: *My Paris* by Doisnau, *Edward Weston's Youths, New Color* by Harry Callahan, *The Changing Face of America* by Peter C. Jones, *Pictures of People* by Nicholas Nixon, *Some Towns* by George Tyce, *Italy: Seasons of Light* by Michael Ruetz, Robert Mapplethorpe's *Some Women.*

Steven checks the Mapplethorpe for a publication date, just to make sure it isn't a first edition *after* the artist's death. That would make a difference. But it isn't. He notices that the introduction was written by Joan Didion.

"You know," he says, relating the kind of book trivia that he loves, "if you find a signed Joan Didion, it's very good. She has agoraphobia, and she doesn't come out in public. She goes to very few signings."

After the photographic books have been lined up, the hardback fiction and nonfiction come next. *Sylvia Beach and the Lost Generation* by Noel Riley Fitch, James Dickey's *Wayfarer*, as well as novels by Graham Swift, Geoffrey Moorehouse, Jane Smiley, Penelope Lively, and a golf joke book.

"I'm glad that this happened now," Steven says. "If it was later I would have all sorts of problems."

Because of the time needed here, he will have to cut short his itinerary for the rest of the morning, and he won't be able do the last blocks to the north or the buildings that he wanted to return to by seven A.M. As it is, he already has too much in his trolley. The Sotheby's and Christie's catalogs that he started the morning with are now taking up much-needed space. If he didn't have them, he would be able to fit in more. Since the catalogs are sold on eBay, and there's no hurry to get them to a bookstore, he decides to dispose of them—not in the trash, but in a hiding place.

"I stash them till later in the day, when I can come back and pick them up."

Steven leaves the books for a few minutes and wheels his trolley with the catalogs to the nearest corner, where there are three or four plastic bins for free newspaper handouts like the *Resident*. He stops in front of the *Jewish Sentinel*, which is his hiding place.

"This is how I move lots of stuff," he says. "No one ever looks in there."

On opening the bin, however, he finds that someone else has already stowed away a dozen romance novels. It could be another book dealer or one of Mr. Murphy's canner friends who's diversifying. Steven thoughtlessly sweeps the novels aside and shoves in every last catalog.

Once he has returned to the books on the sidewalk—which he does quickly, before any passerby can think of grabbing one of his neatly arranged titles—and has fitted them into his trolley, it is past seven A.M. A sanitation truck moves along the street, and it doesn't take long for the plastic bags and boxes that Steven usually goes for to disappear.

As we walk, Steven gives a cursory look at various piles that haven't been taken yet, and he pauses for a while to flip through the old *Life* magazines about Kennedy and the moon landing, but at this point he will take something only if it's truly fantastic. His gait is more relaxed now, and he seems pleased with his haul.

The Strand bookstore, Steven's favorite place to sell books, opens at nine A.M., so he has more than an hour to fill. And knowing him, he will fill that hour most productively. He leads the way to a thrift store on Seventieth Street, where he regularly helps them sort books—and, at the same time, buys whatever he wants before anyone else can get it.

An hour later, he is at the subway station. He weaves his trolley in and out of the early-morning crowds heading to work, until he reaches the far end of the platform. Everything is carefully choreographed so that when he reaches Union Square, he will be at the right staircase to make his exit. In time, Steven will alter this routine and make it much simpler and streamlined. He will take a cab.

On the train, people don't know what to make of him (street collector or book collector?), and you can see that they aren't sure whether to shift away from him or check if he's got a title they might want. By the time we get to the Strand, on lower Broadway, five men and one woman with trolleys have already gathered at the back entrance. Steven doesn't say anything to them, doesn't make eye contact, even though he knows exactly who they are—the competition. You can see he doesn't consider any of them a threat.

"The good thing is that a lot of the guys who do this don't read or know anything about books. They know an art book, a big shiny cover."

The trouble is, there are more and more of them. In the year that I get to know Steven, the number of book collectors doubles. "It's like a swarm of locusts coming through," he says, echoing the sentiments of Eddie the Soda Can King. Even though they don't know much about books, they take everything in sight. Then there is the man who drives around in a Mercedes-Benz and somehow always turns up where Steven has found something.

"We always land up in a shouting match," he says.

The books that the people outside the Strand have are mysteries, novels with tattered covers, and titles that Steven would flatly reject. He picks up a book from the morning's collecting, titled *Chatauqua—A Center for Education, Religion and Arts in America* by Theodore Morrison, and holds it in the direction of the other collectors, as if he is pointing out the difference between them and himself.

"They don't realize that there are people looking for books about Chatauqua."

When it is Steven's turn to go into the store to have his books appraised, he has the titles arranged in the order that he believes will get him the best price. First go the hardbacks, nonfiction and fiction; second, the art books; and last, the paperbacks.

"It creates a good impression. They think from the start that you have good stuff."

The man behind the counter doesn't acknowledge Steven, the same way Steven didn't acknowledge his competitors. There's a quiet recognition of each other. No one is saying where the books came from and no one is asking. The buyer takes each book as if he isn't interested in it, moves it from one side of the counter to the other like a croupier moving chips that don't belong to him, his face not once betraying an emotion. Then, fifty-seven books later, he tells Steven what he will give him. He doesn't even pause to think about it: two hundred dollars.

Steven thinks that's pretty good for a morning's work, and it doesn't even include the catalogs. Which reminds him, as he pulls his trolley out of the store and heads north, that he still has to fetch the catalogs before midday. Afterward, as always, he will take a nap.

chapter 7

the voyeur

If there is such a thing as a latent collecting gene, Christiana's was triggered on Labor Day, 1997. As she was taking her dog for a morning walk, she noticed a man pulling a computer from between some trash cans. He wasn't collecting garbage but simply boasting to his friends about what great stuff could be found on the streets of New York.

Christiana, it so happened, was looking for a computer. Even though she already owned an Apple, she had recently started up as a consultant and needed a computer that was IBM-compatible. She didn't want to spend a lot on one, although it had never occurred to her that she might get it for free.

As soon as the man put the PC back on the sidewalk and left, she went over and inspected it for herself. It was a Compaq and was in good condition—with a CD, a hard drive, and a 28.8 modem. She didn't take it immediately, but went home, thought about it, hurried back before the sanitation trucks could get it, and then carried it the four blocks home.

The computer didn't work when she plugged it in, so she tried to fix it. She didn't know much about PCs, but that didn't deter her. Years earlier when she bought her first computer, a Mac LC, she had set it up on her own and had later figured out how to install more RAM and a new hard drive.

Using some parts she received from a friend, she got the Compaq running. It had sixteen megabytes of RAM, although the software had been erased, the hard drive had been reformatted, and the machine had its quirks. In order to function, its cable had to be draped several inches across the front of the monitor, and there was an IBM logo permanently onscreen.

Nothing she did could get the mouse to work, but trying to fix it gave her plenty of opportunity to acquaint herself with the machine. She got used to DOS and Windows. She checked the computer's bios for ports and interrupt settings, and bought a Windows update to find out how the components interacted with the operating system. When she finally resorted to calling Microsoft's support line for help, she felt as if there was nothing the technician at the other end could tell her that she hadn't deduced for herself. And she was right.

"I knew as much as he did and had already done everything he was telling me to do. He couldn't solve the problem, either, so he said there must be a problem with the motherboard."

To get a replacement motherboard, Christiana once again took to the streets. Seeing as computer parts are interchangeable, she quickly found a usable motherboard, although once it had been installed the mouse still didn't work and she gave up on the Compaq. But she didn't give up on other discarded computers. Now that she had pried open one operating system and had found it wasn't too hard to understand, she wanted to try more. She compares it to putting together a gigantic puzzle. If the biggest thrill for most collectors is finding an object, for Christiana that is only where the adventure starts.

"It's not like fixing a car, which is all mechanical," she says. "Here there's an operating system you need to know in order to make work. Without that, it's just a piece of junk. You have to be very logical and decide a whole series of steps to find out why it's not working."

Her two-bedroom apartment slowly started filling up with hard drives and monitors, for both PCs and Apples, and after a year of collecting, Christiana, who is in her early forties, started selling the fixed machines. She charges several hundred dollars for an entire system—computer, monitor, printer—and the installation. Anything less than 150 megahertz or older than two years she rejects.

Christiana doesn't earn enough off the computers to make a living, but that was never the point. From the very beginning, she collected in order to educate herself. The sidewalk taught her not only about PCs and software programs but also about networking, and it has been a more effective school than a real one. Several of her acquaintances began studying computers in college at the same time she started collecting them, but she has already learned far more. And besides the few things she's had to purchase—parts and manuals that she generally buys from the black-bag people she meets out collecting or who sell stuff on the sidewalks of Harlem—her education has cost her almost nothing.

"I have learned enough by now to get a computer-related job," she says.

This nuts-and-bolts (or rather, this gigabytes-and-RAM) attitude is what initially attracted me to Christiana. Every facet of her collecting had a reason—why she collects, what she collects, and what she's going to do with it—and she believed that as soon as she accomplished her goal of getting a full-time job working with computers in an office, she would stop doing it. She never took things off the sidewalk before that

Labor Day in 1997, and she could see a time soon when she would give it up. Like Jeffrey, it was a phase of her life, and she could turn it off like a faucet.

But something totally unexpected happened to Christiana, something that she couldn't have foreseen when she brought home that very first Compaq. And now, even though she won't admit it, giving up computers might not be that easy.

The morning I met Christiana for the first time, I had left home early with the intention of carrying out an experiment. I wanted to see if I could actually furnish an apartment with all the mongo I spotted in several hours. I didn't exactly fill all the rooms, but I got pretty close.

For the living room there was an Andrew Wyeth print, a radiator cover, an old rug, nice cushions, a brass-and-glass coffee table, glass shelves, a three-tiered corner table, curtain material, a bridge table with leather inlay, and a modern mantelpiece; for the bedroom, cane blinds, a bedframe, a mattress from a whole variety (old, new, or futon), an unhealthy-looking palm, and a nice bookcase; for the kitchen, a Formica table, a refrigerator, a stepladder, a vacuum cleaner (out of a choice of five), a kitchen cupboard, and mops galore; for the bathroom, a large wall mirror with a slightly chipped frame and a wicker laundry basket missing a handle; for the office, a two-drawer filing cabinet, a desk and a swivel chair (out of a choice of six); and for the yard, several wicker potholders, a garden umbrella, and a huge pottery urn.

The things I saw that I couldn't find any use for in my make-believe home included a baby stroller, crutches, two kid's bikes, four suitcases, six drawers without their chest, and several thousand copies of brand-new yellow pages still wrapped in plastic.

If I felt any sense of accomplishment at finding so many things with which to fill an imaginary apartment, it was offset by my disappointment that no one was actually collecting them. It was like having a secret to tell but no one to tell it to. The few people out at five in the morning were walking their dogs, while the three collectors I came across were focusing on other things: cans, black bags, and toys.

The two Mexican women who were searching for toys seemed to be onto an interesting kind of mongo, but as soon as I approached them to find out more, they took the course of many collectors I approached on the street. They fled. As they tore down the block, someone came in the opposite direction pulling a trolley. It was Christiana, and she was visibly excited about her latest find, which sat propped up in her trolley, a two-year-old, 450-megahertz Gateway Pentium II. It had a DVD drive, a CD player, a Zip drive, a 10-gigabyte hard drive, and a 64-megabyte DIMM memory—several hundred dollars' worth of parts she could sell if the computer didn't work—but that wasn't the best thing about it. The Gateway was also in very good shape.

Most of the components Christiana finds come in pieces. She has never figured out who disassembles them, their owners, the maintenance people who put out the garbage, or salvagers in search of copper wire and pieces of gold. The only items she regularly comes across that haven't been dismantled are monitors. And even when a computer is left whole, its condition can vary from fairly unscathed to severely damaged. One model was so battered, it looked as if someone had repeatedly hit it with a sledgehammer, clearly wanting to ensure that no one ever got any information or service from it again. Only that person hadn't counted on Christiana finding it.

After she saved the motherboard, which she used elsewhere, she proceeded to find out who the last owner was. She could do this because the sledgehammer hadn't done the trick. A more effective method would have been for him to have erased the hard drive, although even that isn't fail-safe—at least not when Christiana is involved. She can unerase hard drives, and it has now become an integral part of her collecting routine to do so. For it turns out that half the fun of finding a computer is finding out who threw it away.

It's as if prying open the system begs her to pry open its history too. If she doesn't, her discovery remains incomplete. Whose mind, she wants to know, lies behind the blank screen she just found? Who created the problems that she just solved? And who thought that he could get the better of her by trying to obliterate his background with a blow from a heavy object?

So when Christiana says that "each computer is like a person," she means two things. Each computer, like someone in distress, can be helped if you give it enough love and care, and each computer contains all the elements of an individual. "It's like meeting a new person," she says. "There's always a piece of someone's life."

In this way Christiana has "met" doctors, bookkeepers, lawyers, teachers, and schoolchildren who can't write or spell properly. A psychiatrist left behind all his medical programs, including one on how to evaluate whether people are crazy, which, for fun, she took. A writer didn't erase his short stories, some of them extremely personal, which she read. On an economist's computer, she discovered his tax information for the previous five years, his social security number, his financial background, and his résumé.

Reading the intimate stories and the psychiatrist's files didn't make her feel guilty, but the mundane information left by the economist did. Her immediate impulse was to phone him up, ask if he wanted the computer back, and warn him to be more careful in the future. But before she could, another collector advised her not to.

"He said the man would only become more afraid if he knew that a stranger had all this information about him. In the end, I erased everything."

To me, these strangers' lives are as much a kind of mongo as the computers they're on. They are like the Communion photograph of the old Italian that Jeffrey found on Allen Street, or the male pornography that Steven found tucked between the Catholic literature of a football-playing Notre Dame alumnus. They are shreds of a private life that someone, by putting them out with the garbage, has unwittingly agreed to share with the passing trade.

Christiana doesn't agree at all, and I get the impression that she finds me frivolous for even making the suggestion. Nor does she like the idea of people finding out that she does this, especially those people whose computers she has explored. She knows so much about her cyberacquaintances—their names, addresses, birthdays, possibly even their favorite kinky Web sites—that she can pick them out on the streets of her neighborhood, and even though I promise to mask her identity, she believes they will recognize her too.

Not once during our conversations does Christiana admit something that seems quite obvious: She reads the files of strangers because she's curious. And yet snooping is an inextricable element of collecting, as most collectors readily acknowledge. Guessing the identity of a previous owner of something they've found is an automatic reflex. Even when there's not much to go on, collectors speculate. Sarah makes up her own stories. Steven imagines the kind of people inside a building from the quality of literature and papers outside. Other collectors ascribe qualities to people from their garbage, be it the fact that they throw out gifts that haven't even been unwrapped (mean), they eat lots of fast food despite living at a wealthy address (lazy or miserly), or hide porn magazines between dull files (sneaky). Christiana, meanwhile, has much more information to go on than any other collector; it's literally at her fingertips. All she has to do is fix the computer and open up the files. By unerasing the ones that have purposely been deleted she can go even further and dig even deeper. But that part of her treasure map she suddenly withdraws from me, ending our meetings as abruptly as the linen woman from Greenwich did.

Depending on whom you ask, this second side of Christiana's collecting could be seen as innocent fun, voyeurism, or a crime. On the economist's computer were three key elements—his name, birth date, and social security number—that could have been used to access his credit history and to then go on a spending spree with his money. Christiana might not have wanted to do that, but lots of people would.

Identity theft is the fastest growing crime in the country. The Federal Trade Commission estimates that in 2002 there were almost ten million victims of this fraud, costing financial institutions about forty-eight billion dollars. Why identity theft is so popular, according to police, is its simplicity. The act is anonymous, you don't need to break into anyone's home to do it, and you don't even have to be seen. All that's required is a person's vital information, which can be obtained in countless ways, whether it's taken from a lost wallet or copied from the records in a doctor's office. As far as getting it out of the trash goes, the only source more popular than a discarded computer is discarded paper.

It was recently discovered that a man in San Diego was paying fifty dollars for every bag of dry garbage that was brought to him. In his garage, police found countless documents that he had sorted into different piles, which were then used to create fake identities and sold in batches of ten. From this enterprise he could make up to a thousand dollars a week. It's not known how many cases of identity theft begin in a trash can, but enough for the term *Dumpster diving* to have come to suggest a very different kind of lawlessness from the one the food collectors espouse.

The incident in San Diego was one of the few to have been recorded or solved. In spite of the scope of the crime of identity theft, it gets hardly any publicity, mostly because there's little to publicize. The credit industry keeps quiet, fearing that this kind of bad news could provoke new laws making credit less easily accessible; victims seldom know how their identity got stolen in the first place, or, if they do, are too embarrassed or scared to admit it; and if an imposter gets caught, which rarely happens, he is unlikely to disclose his methods. All the FTC can do for the time being is caution people to shred their financial records and, in a move that will severely curb Christiana's routine, to wipe out all personal information on their computers with a "kill" program that makes files unrecoverable.

Even though Christiana and I never spoke about identity theft, she was the person who indirectly led me to it. Which surprised me. I would have expected to learn about this underbelly of collecting from Steven or Mr. Murphy, someone with more street smarts. Yet from the very start, Christiana contradicted every notion I had of a street collector, even the way she dressed. Not that street collectors have a particular uniform, but they usually prepare themselves for dirt when they head out. Christiana, on the other hand, always wore a clean pair of slacks and a nice bright shirt, maybe an anorak to keep off the morning chill, and her hair looked like it could have been cut a few days earlier. She was more uptown housewife than someone down on her luck.

Her routine wasn't what you'd expect from a collector, either, for she emerged from her apartment in Chelsea only after daybreak, which isn't the worst time to search for mongo, but it's pretty bad; the best stuff has probably been taken throughout the night. She did this, she claimed, because she felt safer when it was light outside, and yet she wouldn't think twice about wandering deep into Harlem to check out the things being sold by the black-bag guys, who have even offered to sell her guns.

Her motivation was distinctive too; she was one of the few people I met besides the food collectors who believed quite fervently in recycling. Yet when I asked her why she thought other people collected, she didn't give recycling as one of the reasons. Perhaps she thought that recyclers were such an insignificant sector of this community (and she's probably right) that they weren't worth mentioning.

"People collect," she said, "because they are crazy or they want to avoid dying."

The reply came so quickly, it was obvious that she had thought about the subject before, and she didn't include herself in either group. When she mentioned craziness, I immediately thought she'd discovered some connection between collecting and dementia when she took the test on the psychiatrist's computer. But then I realized that she was merely identifying the two main groups of collectors she comes across most often: the ones she sees on the sidewalk, collecting cans or going through black bags, who talk to themselves and shake their fists at her; and the ones she sees in stores, who keep buying more and more things (which is really just collecting in disguise) when they already have enough.

"People go out and buy two or three homes and redecorate them," she told me. "It doesn't make any sense why we have so many possessions. You see that on the street when people redecorate and they throw out everything. Why do we have to have the latest of everything? Why are we into possessions? It's got something to do with death."

Putting a label on any collector is as unwise as it is impossible, for there are as many reasons why they collect as what they collect and how. There is collecting for business, treasure, education, a political statement, theft, historical preservation, entertainment, necessity, a meal ticket. The words I'd choose to describe the collectors I met would be *fun, clever, funny, interesting, weird, exceptionally bright,* but not, as far as I could tell, *crazy* and certainly not *death-fearing.* Like anyone, they have their share of problems. Dave admitted that collecting hadn't helped his love life, but otherwise he was having a good time. Steven disliked the way people treated him, but both he and Mr. Murphy were certainly happier than they had ever been in an office. Sarah had been through several bad marriages, but collecting had been a mainstay through it all. In fact, the only people who might have had death on their minds were the food collectors, and that would have been not their own but those of all globalizing, industrializing capitalists.

Yet it turns out that Christiana is partly right. Collectors, and this refers to collectors of anything, sometimes do collect as a hedge against mortality. A psychiatrist who works at Bellevue Hospital in New York, Dr. Ricardo Castaneda, says that, for some people, collecting can create a feeling of permanence, and they believe that in their collection they are leaving behind something of themselves when they die. An art collection left for posterity could quite possibly be someone's attempt to achieve immortality. William Randolph Hearst, one of the most famous collectors of all time, who bought so many artworks and artifacts that he didn't have enough space for them in his many mansions, was said to have been equally obsessed by collecting as by death.

A fear of death, it has been suggested, was also what motivated the most infamous collectors of mongo, the Collyer brothers. Homer and Langley Collyer grew up and lived in a brownstone in Harlem in the early twentieth century. Both of them went to college, where they studied law and medicine, but neither ever worked. After their mother died in 1929, they lived on their own in the brownstone, both by that stage eccentric, reclusive, and in their forties. The water, gas, and electricity were eventually cut off, and the brothers boarded up the windows. Langley was seen only when he went out scavenging late at night, while Homer, plagued by illness and eventually blindness, remained indoors.

In 1947, the police responded to a tip-off that there might

be something amiss at the Collyer home. After no one answered the front door, they broke in, only to be confronted by room after room of so much junk that they could barely make their way through. When the contents of the house were later removed, they were calculated to weigh 136 tons and included more than a dozen grand pianos, a horse's jawbone, thousands of medical and engineering books, an old X-ray machine, the chassis of a Model T Ford, gas chandeliers, part of a horse carriage, mannequins, and more than six tons of newspapers. Crawl spaces had been dug through it all and had been booby-trapped to deter intruders.

Both brothers were dead, although the police could find only Homer at first. An invalid by that stage, he had apparently been unable to reach food. It took another two weeks to find Langley. Even though his body lay only ten feet away from his brother, it was covered in junk, which had toppled onto him when one of the booby-trapped tunnels collapsed. The sellable goods from the house were put on auction, fetching a total of only eighteen hundred dollars, and after the place was emptied, it was demolished.

Whether the Collyers suffered from a fear of death (or, as has also been suggested, a fear of poverty, schizophrenia, obsessive-compulsive behavior, or even addiction), or whether they were just hoarders, their story is regarded today more as weird than as cautionary. And yet New York is still home to many people like them. Dr. Castaneda says he has seen numerous cases that compare to the Collyers but that have never been publicized. One woman has a six-story brownstone packed full of newspapers. The book collector that Steven knew had a building filled with books that he refused to give away, even when they were being removed by men with shovels.

The only hoarder I met was a woman named Mary—and I call her a hoarder instead of, say, a pack rat, because it's the term psychiatrists seem to prefer to describe people who collect with almost reckless abandon. But Mary managed to keep her pastime so well concealed that I never even knew she was a collector until several months after our last meeting. A dear woman in her sixties, she dedicated almost all her time to taking in homeless cats, which she had neutered and inoculated, before she tried to find them homes. All of this she paid for with her own money.

I first came across Mary in a pet store, where she had a tabby and a calico up for adoption. When I mentioned that there were some stray cats in my neighborhood, she implored me to catch them for her. Over the next few months I caught five, and each time I went to drop one off at her apartment, she would be waiting on the sidewalk, an empty cage in hand, and she'd coo words of affection to the new arrival. I always took her preparedness as a sign of her dedication, but it was probably because she didn't want anyone getting too close to her apartment. Even on the sidewalk you could smell old cat pee coming from the building, but that was only a small indication of what was going on inside.

When Mary had a stroke one summer, an acquaintance who'd known her for many years finally got into the apartment and uncovered her secret. She not only rescued cats, she collected them. About two hundred cats were stored in her apartment as well as in five other apartments in the building. Mary could do this because she owned the building. As her acquaintance pointed out to me, Mary probably could have financed quite a respectable cat-rescue operation with what she earned off rentals, but she made hardly anything off the building. Half the apartments had cats in them, and in the other half were tenants who refused to pay rent because of the stench.

The horrific scene that confronted the woman who discovered the cats sickened her more than anything she'd ever seen. Some of the animals were dead, and the rest were either badly emaciated or their front paws had become foreshortened from being kept in the stacked cages for so long. Nor was that where Mary's collecting ended. Her apartment was also filled with garbage, old clothes, and hundreds of full bottles of Coca-Cola. So much junk had been piled in the bathroom that it could no longer be reached, so Mary had started using the kitchen floor as a toilet.

"She had no control over what she was doing anymore," said her friend.

Mary was not crazy, at least not according to a psychologist I spoke with afterward, but she was quite possibly addicted to collecting. The psychologist, Elizabeth Fagan, who has worked with psychotic street collectors, told me that Mary probably started rescuing cats with the very best of intentions. Her initial good deed could have been so satisfying, though, that she just kept on doing it. When she couldn't find homes for the cats fast enough, she didn't stop collecting them; she stored them.

"What happens with an addiction is that the thing—the pot, the ring, the cat—makes you feel good for a certain amount of time," Fagan explained. "But it becomes an addiction when you start walking away from other things that can also give you a good feeling about yourself. You start shutting down other areas of your life." Or, as Dr. Castaneda put it, each time a collector finds something, there is a gratifying physical sensation. And a desire for that feeling is what sets him or her off the next time around.

"It's like a fetish or sexual arousal," he said. "You want to re-create that. You want to reactivate that pleasant emotion."

The psychology of collecting is a little-studied field, and even Freud, who himself collected art, stayed away from it. What motivates collectors of any kind could be passion, obsession, or addiction, but it is rarely a psychosis. Where sickness does enter the picture, according to Dr. Castaneda, is in cities like New York, where mentally ill people who are cut off by their families congregate and find a home on the street, often resorting to cans or black bags to support themselves. The disease they suffer from most often is schizophrenia, a condition that is aggravated among at least 65 percent of them by an addiction to alcohol or cocaine.

Mr. Murphy had told me about the unbalanced canners, and numerous other collectors besides Christiana had remarked about their colleagues they believed were crazy. Drugs were often mentioned in the same breath, but never schizophrenia, and I'm not sure anyone really knew what caused these collectors' strange behavior of muttering to themselves, screaming, flailing their hands. After talking to Dr. Castaneda, I realized that the mentally ill didn't choose mongo, but that it chose them, for it allowed them to buy food, liquor, and drugs, making it in many cases an inadvertent bridge between sickness and addiction.

As different as these people are from sludgers and finders and pickers and Dumpster divers, I still believed that they made up an intrinsic part of the story of street collecting. But Dr. Castaneda warned me that even if I could find such people willing to talk to me, they would come up with all kinds of delusional explanations for their behavior. That was certainly the case with Gloria, whom I befriended despite the doctor's better judgment.

The first thing that struck me about Gloria wasn't that she was crazy—a psychotic schizophrenic, in fact—but her infectious laugh and gold snaggletooth. She was sitting on a bench at the edge of Central Park, and in spite of the summer heat, she was wearing a thick winter jacket, several layers of scarves, and swathes of dark material. Her shopping cart was typical canner, with clothes, plastic bags, and a bottle of Evian.

As I approached her I noticed that she was scribbling in a notebook. When I asked if she was a collector, she immediately began explaining that she was working on a theory. She had a roundabout way of saying things, be it her age ("I'm at a thirty-two-year balance") or her marital status ("It depends on where you are in the universe"), while her story kept changing (I counted at least twelve professions, including pilot, medical engineer, housewife, architect, lieutenant on a spaceship, and taxi driver), and she made up phrases that sounded quite impressive but meant nothing, such as "evaluationary scales," "medical attainment levels," and "fractionary codes."

Around her daily activity of pushing her cart up and down the avenues, she had built a kind of sci-fi fable. Familiar things acquired new identities. The entrances to Central Park became the Five Thousand Gates, while the Stretch was that part of Fifth Avenue where you were most likely to find cans. Her clothes, or street rags, as she called them, were actually a uniform given to her by the military, where she worked as a lieutenant. Normally the uniform was white, but because her job of "entering tunnels and pulling switches" dirtied her clothes so much, street rags were more advisable. Gloria also lived by two codes, the military and the universal. She laughed at me when I admitted that I didn't know what they were and when I expressed total ignorance of what a deep-sea firefighter and "developmental process levels" were.

Not surprisingly, garbage itself received numerous identities, but most important it was a means for her to carry out scientific experiments. The endless rows of small, symmetrical figures I had seen her writing in her notepad were meant to be her theories on the weight of rays, giving rise to her final and most important profession of beam doctor. There was also garbage as psychological ammunition ("A husband and wife throw mental garbage at each other") and garbage found not because you were on the lookout for it but because God was ("He was answering your brain"). When Gloria finally talked about garbage as garbage, you could see that she had a deep-seated respect for it, as if it were one of the most important subsections of her military and universal codes.

"I don't say *garbage* anymore, I say *sanitation*," she said, "because I done learnt my categories of sanitation. I done learnt certain factors in association to dealing with garbage. I know how to decalculate the garbage, how to store the garbage, how to refine the garbage, how to recycle the garbage, et cetera. I don't look at a bottle anymore as just being a bottle, I look at it as being five cents."

Gloria's whimsical world of the Five Thousand Gates was, as far as I could make out, a wild collection of ideas mixed up with the things she saw and heard every day, such as the blare of sirens, the hospital across the road, the posters on passing buses, as well as the sometimes horrible truth of her daily pattern of sleeping on park benches, being arrested, having her fingerprints taken, being beaten up at night. The resulting tale sounded a lot less hellish than it probably was.

On a typical day, then, she would come out of the Third Gate and head for the Stretch, where she sometimes preferred "to do automotives," her way of saying cleaning windscreens. She would follow "guidelines" and "guidemarks" on the Stretch, and later she would make sure to rendezvous with the Courier at the "junctionary time points." If she didn't, she was required to have her fingerprints taken. Once, when she forgot to meet the Courier, the military came to fetch her, descending from all sides, their sirens blaring. They told her that it was essential for her to have a military escort by her side at all times or there could be serious consequences.

"If I should get hurt," she explained, "if something was to happen to me, the level of money is extreme—we're talking about, in the military system, because I started off as a military child in terms of creation as a beam doctor, if I was to get hurt on a spaceship, it's something like . . . I think the highest was something like eight hundred trillion dollars."

Gloria suddenly broke off her explanation to scream at a passing dog, whose owner quickened his pace at the sound of her voice. It was a reaction I had seen countless times before, the civilian dread of a collector who might be a lunatic. In this case, he was right, even though she wasn't going to hurt him. When I asked what her tirade was all about, she explained quite matter-of-factly that dogs also had duties onboard her spaceship, and that this particular dog had let its hair get too long and woolly. She laughed again, flashed her snaggletooth, and then began describing how pushing a shopping cart was, in fact, a very good training exercise to prepare you for the military.

I never saw Gloria again after that, even though I looked for her. I wanted to thank her for letting me linger for a few hours in a strange world that other collectors like her probably also concoct but never let anyone enter. Then again, maybe she wouldn't have understood.

chapter 8

the archaeologists

On the rim of a deep hole in the backyard of a Greenwich Village brownstone lie a series of articles that date back to the mid-1800s. Making up the circle are a section of a five-gallon demijohn wine bottle, a shard from a flowerpot, several marbles, a rubber dog bone, the skeleton of a rodent, and lots of seeds—celery, watermelon, and strawberry.

The latest item Scott hands up from eight feet down is an unbroken piece of curved glass with a tiny perforation in one end that fits snugly into the palm of his hand. Dan, who is standing at the top of the pit, takes the glass from Scott and inspects it.

"It's not a toy," he concludes, although they often find fragments of olden-day playthings at the depth they've reached now. After pausing for a moment, he adds, "And it's definitely not a bottle."

Scott by this stage has pulled himself up to ground level by means of a rope that's hanging from an elementary wooden A-frame contraption straddling the mouth of the hole. He takes the glass from Dan.

"I've seen one of these before," he says, a smirk on his face. He goes into an intricate explanation of how the glass is only one part of the original object, and that there was once a rubber doohickey that would fit over the perforation, and that a woman who had recently given birth would fit the glass to her body in a certain way in order to extract milk. At that point, Dan guffaws.

"It's a breast pump!"

Dan normally has a ribald sense of humor, so the breast pump is to him like, well, mother's milk to a baby. He makes several remarks about being busted and then motions to the vicinity of his chest. His girlfriend, Maya, stands to one side, purposely not smiling even though she wants to.

The commotion over the breast pump attracts the attention of a woman in the house next door, who is sticking her head out of a window on the first floor. She's just high enough to see over the fence, and it's clear that she has been watching Scott and Dan for several minutes already. When the laughing dies down, she calls out, "Are you guys digging the cistern?"

"No," they shout back almost in unison, "the privy."

Under his breath, Scott says to me, "That's a nice way of saying the shithouse."

The privy they're excavating is located in the garden of a home on Jane Street in Greenwich Village. For the most part, Scott and Dan focus on the Village, Chelsea, and SoHo, even though there are privies all around Manhattan, Brooklyn, and Queens.

"Twenty years ago, every backyard in New York City was provided with one of these [privy] buildings," George Waring wrote in his book *Earth-Closets and Earth Sewage*, published in 1870, more than twenty years before he would gain fame as the head of the city's sanitation department. "Now, since the water-closet has come into universal use, probably there are not twenty of them to the square mile."

With all due respect to Waring, Scott believes that the switch from privy to water closet happened more gradually, because people didn't take quickly to the idea of having toilets inside their houses. Scott reads so much about the history of New York, especially in very old, out-of-print books, that he's probably right. Just to be on the safe side, though, and to make sure he and Dan are going to find a privy, they don't target any house built later than 1860.

When a privy did finally fall into disuse, it was covered in one or more materials—ash, soil, stone, rubble—depending on the neighborhood. Much later on came the gardens, the fertilizer, the concrete. And now not many people know that the toilets used to be outside, in the back of the house, and hardly anyone bothers to go look for them. Scott and Dan, as far as they know, are the only private individuals in Manhattan who seek privies out and then open them up.

"You're the guys I heard about," the woman next door calls back.

"Yeah, from Perry Street."

Scott and Dan dug up the privy behind a brownstone on Perry Street two years earlier. The house was owned by Stewart Johnson, one of the heirs of Johnson & Johnson. They still talk about it as their best privy ever, delivering, among other things, two hundred bottles, many of them valuable and one in particular worth one thousand dollars. The Jane Street privy doesn't look nearly as promising.

"Yeah, that's us," says Scott.

"Don't you want to come and do mine?" she asks.

Scott and Dan look at each other. They can't believe their luck. They have been eyeing the neighboring garden off and on throughout the morning. It's a bit forlorn, although that's no sign of what might lie underneath it. The area where they suspect the privy would be is massed in ivy and some heavy brickwork, all of which would have to be lifted and put back again.

"Sure, we could come around and talk to you," says Scott. His voice is even, as if he's used to this kind of request being made every day of the week. He doesn't let on how hard it is to get someone to let them excavate a perfectly fine garden and search for something that might not even be there.

"At first, they're interested," Scott explains later, once they've made a date with the woman to come check out her garden and Dan has climbed down into the shaft. "But when you arrive, they get scared. After the first day they see the hole and then they say, 'Fill it up again.'"

Sometimes they're lucky, and a property owner's initial reservation disappears quickly. Scott and some friends from Colorado got permission to enter a yard in a less affluent Philadelphia suburb, even though the owner wasn't actually sure she wanted to let them dig. At first their request struck her as odd, and she was convinced they were government agents. When Scott pointed out that the paving in her garden had sunk and a sumac tree was growing through the depression—which was a good sign, seeing trees for some reason like privies—she let them break earth. After the first bottle came up, she was hooked. For the entire day she stayed close by, intrigued, and even brought them soft drinks.

Digs in Manhattan seldom happen that smoothly. In the past four years Scott and Dan have managed to persuade only twenty people in the city to let them excavate their yards. Which is also how long the two have been intermittent partners. Sometimes they go out on their own too, or team up with other people, but on digs inside the city it's usually just the two of them. Maya, Dan's girlfriend, has been allowed to come along on this dig because she helped them get the site.

To get potential "clients" on their side, Scott and Dan arrive thoroughly prepared. They bring photos not only of what they've found in other privies but also of how the gardens look after they've been reassembled. They provide articles that have been written about them in antique-bottle magazines, some of which, admittedly, Scott himself has penned. Even so, it took a year to convince the owner of the Jane Street house to let them in.

"I kept calling and he never replied," says Dan. "In the end, he said we were persistent, that's why he let us do it."

A more typical response has come from a few blocks away. A couple found some shells in their garden that they think might be from an old Indian village. The wife wants Scott to come in, but the husband doesn't. He works from home and believes that this kind of operation in his yard would force him to have the place cordoned off and his business closed for a month or more. Scott shakes his head in disbelief.

"He has this weird image of what can be done if something important is found on your property."

Dan laughs at the suggestion. Cordoning off an area? Taking six weeks? Him and Scott? Never. They try to get in and out in forty-eight hours.

"We are just artists and historians having a bunch of fun," he says.

The Jane Street privy is barely five feet in diameter, more compact than many that they have done in Manhattan. The ladder takes up a lot of the cavity, so whoever is down below has to work his way around it. Privies can go to double this one's size and can be as deep as twenty feet, thirty feet in

Philadelphia. Dan says one pit was so large they had four people in it at once, and it was comfortable enough down there to spend an hour or two drinking beers. They even wanted to sleep inside it one night so they could get an early start the next morning, but in the end they didn't.

Wide or narrow, most New York privies are lined in stone and cone outward the deeper they get, with the entrance made purposely small so that a shack could sit safely on top and wouldn't fall in when its wooden base started rotting. The bigger the cone, the bigger the potential for what's inside.

Now that Dan is in the hole, it's Scott's turn to haul dirt. At the end of the rope that Scott used to climb to the surface is a plastic bucket for extracting the privy's innards. In this slow, painstaking fashion, they will remove more than thirty thousand pounds of soil, ash, fossilized feces. And they hope that among it all, there will be something of value.

"Sometimes people would throw anything into the outhouse," says Scott. "Things would also be dropped in by mistake."

What they're hoping for, more than anything else, is bottles— old, intact, and unscratched. Whatever each one finds, he keeps. If it's something good, they immediately switch jobs until the next good thing comes up. All in all, it's very fair, very just.

In the same way, they are fair to the person whose property they're on, promising them one third of anything that comes up. They admittedly don't pay for the right to dig, and they have plenty of time to remove the best artifacts before anyone else gets a chance, but few property owners seem particularly interested in owning anything that's exhumed. The kick for them, it seems, is the dig itself.

Stewart Johnson has never claimed his third—which includes

seventeen bottles, a crock, and an intact porcelain doll—and Scott keeps it stored in his apartment, in spite of the fact that he can't even fit in some of his own things anymore. The rooms are already so crowded with privy finds that he has taken to hiding the bigger bottles elsewhere. He sticks them in the ground upside down on vacant lots and in the river- bank near his apartment. He has no written record of their whereabouts, but he says that doesn't matter.

"I remember where each one is."

Most privies come up in layers. First there's the cover that has accumulated over the years: leaves, garden buildup, and what- ever the owners have added. In this case, that includes a yard full of two-by-fours and rubble from the brownstone, all of which has to be removed before work can begin.

"Generally, the first six feet is kind of quiet," says Scott. "It gets depressing."

Once they have cut through the modern-day layers, they reach coal ash, which in olden times would have been removed from the burners in the nearby house. In some cases there might also be a stratum of a whitish substance called wall debris, a combination of ash, cement, and plaster. But mostly the filler consists of reddish-yellow dirt full of rocks, bricks, and other heavy rubble. Considering the weight and size of the filler, it is surprising that anything below, especially fragile bottles and glass breast pumps, went unharmed.

"The artifacts were preserved in that soft layer underneath," Scott explains. "Because it was very soupy when they dropped in the first rock, objects were cushioned."

Depending on where the privy is, its shape and contents will differ. The older and wealthier a community was, the

better the privy, which means the eastern seaboard and
California hold the best potential for diggers. In Brooklyn,
privies were made smaller and shallower than in Manhattan,
were cleaned more thoroughly, and were filled almost to the
top with ash when they were closed. On Staten Island, they
were lined in wood, and there would be four or five in a
yard—in addition to the garbage pits.

"Staten Island is a difficult place," Scott says. "You bruise
your arms and bones all day, digging and chopping in empty
lots and on construction sites, and you come up with nothing.
You get permission to dig up a backyard, then dig all day,
and come up with a garbage pit that has a few things in it
but no well. It's a strange place."

In Philadelphia, besides going down deeper, the privies were
brick-lined, while in Colorado mining towns like Leadville
they were made of wood or empty barrels placed in the earth
on top of one another. Some diggers out west also search for
privies where old forts used to be, although it is so hard to
find them that an entire foot of a probing rod can be worn
off in a year of searching. In Manhattan, you might use up
an inch of a probe, not to mention that the contents of the
privy will almost certainly be a lot more valuable.

The items that Scott and Dan are after lie in the stratum
of leftover feces, which is also called night soil. This term,
Scott says, originally came not from the people who used the
toilet but from the people who cleaned it.

"They were Irish or black guys, paid a terrible wage to do
the job, a bunch of drunks probably." He gives the kind of
details that sound fabricated, but which in fact he has garnered
from old books and copies of *Valentine's History of New York*,
a magazine dating back to the mid-nineteenth century. "But

from the eighteen-seventies, people were getting these new concepts about diseases and there was a growing controversy about what was causing them. One of the ideas was that the privy diggers—the dippers, the guys who cleaned them out— were creating a lot of diseases, because when they opened them up it stunk like hell. And if it was in the middle of a hot summer . . . you can imagine.

"Eventually people got so paranoid, you'd find them shooting at the dippers, sniping from the rooftops. It got so dangerous to clean the wells that they started doing it at night with armed guards. That's where the term *night soil* comes from—for human waste."

"They were also called honeydippers," adds Dan, smiling at the euphemism, which makes him think of another one. "In Alcatraz, they spoke about the rose garden. If you had to clean all the chamber pots and privies, you emptied them in a place called the rose garden."

One scatological anecdote leads to another, which, given the focus of their work, is inevitable. Who developed the toilet? ("A man named Crapp." "No, it was Crapeur." Laughter.) Which nation had toilets first? (No answer.) Does night soil still smell one hundred and fifty years later?

"No," says Dan. "A privy would lose its smell a year after being covered."

He's talking about Manhattan, of course, where the earth is generally dry. But when Scott dug in Philadelphia, where the water table is higher, he and his friends hit liquid at the halfway mark of fifteen feet. After another two feet, they reached the night soil, which was similar to a black gooey mud and got firmer until it became like peat moss. They eventually reached a fibrous horse manure.

"It was pretty tough to deal with," says Scott, recalling the stench.

The problem was that the night soil, after so many years, was releasing methane, which left them feeling nauseous, dizzy, and light-headed. So even though the privy was a worthwhile one—delivering eighty bottles, some food containers, Victorian jewelry, and several odd-looking clamps that were once used on fruit jars (and which they eventually sold for almost three thousand dollars)—each person could work no longer than forty minutes at a time.

In Manhattan, the only place where the privies could be damp is in a section of the West Village that was once known as Lispenard Meadows, a marshy area used as a dumping ground for just about anything until the eighteenth century. Scott paraphrases a description he read in one of his history books that makes the site sound like it was New York's version of Montfaucon, the infamously foul dumping ground of Paris.

"When you enter Lispenard Meadows," he recalls reading, "it's covered with the refuse and rotting growth of the ages."

Whether or not a privy smells isn't the only thing people are curious about. Other questions that repeatedly get asked are whether Scott and Dan are searching for gold (Answer: "Mostly it's nails if it's metal. Or a buckle") or a body.

"We've had people call the cops on us," Dan says, "even when we had permission to be there. 'We got a call someone's burying a body,' they'll say. We show them articles that have been written about us, the bottles, and eventually the cops will start laughing. It's amazing what human paranoia can create."

No matter how many times the questions get asked, Dan

and Scott answer each one of them politely and thoughtfully. Their attitude is much the same when they go to flea markets to sell some of the privy items. Scott always displays an assortment of standard 1860 and 1870 bottles—puffs, they call them, or shitters—that people can pick up and handle, as well as a board of photos explaining what privy digging is all about. One photo is of Scott in a hole alone; another is of him with Dan, showing off some of the artifacts they found at the Johnson house; and yet another is a close-up of five bottles, each a different color, and all of them, amazingly, dug up unbroken. Scott and Dan see part of their job as educational, and the table and photos could be their version of *A Brief Introduction to New York Privies*.

Neither one of them has any professional training, just dirty-handed experience, which is a fact that irks numerous professionals. New York is a very new site in archaeological terms, and historical excavation in the city began in earnest only in the early 1970s. Most of that work until now has centered on the extreme south of Manhattan, the location of the first settlements and the oldest landfill.

To local archaeologists, privy and landfill diggers are simply looters, destroying priceless history purely for monetary gain. Archaeologist Joan Geismar helped unearth the South Street Seaport area, during which thousands of artifacts were found, including a ship.

"They are systematically wiping out evidence that can be used to put together a portrait of the lifestyles of those people who lived in the houses," she says, "what they ate, drank, the hair tonics they used, the medicines they consumed."

The excavated ship, for example, helped add one very big piece to the puzzle of landfill—that scuttled vessels were used to create massive barriers that would hold back garbage and other landfill ingredients—and has led historians to conclude that quite a few more ships might lie buried under the city.

Before archaeologists can work on a site, however, a long and arduous investigation has to be carried out, after which a final go-ahead must be obtained from the Landmarks Preservation Committee. Privy diggers, meanwhile, go out and solicit sites on their own, and although that process can also take a lot of time, the final decision has nothing to do with committees or public opinion. Archaeologists argue that should those privies ever come up as potential digs, they will be useless, for the earth has been disturbed and the context of what's in the privies destroyed. Not that permission would ever be granted to dig up those privies, seeing as only 1 percent of all applications to the landmarks committee get the green light.

Scott and Dan don't worry about the accusations.

"If archaeologists were here," Dan says, "they'd be here for six weeks. Everything would have a number on it, every piece of every thing."

"The angle they fell apart," adds Scott, sounding like they've had this conversation before. "The distance from each other."

In one of the city's most famous archaeological projects, the Five Points slum that was featured in the movie *Gangs of New York*, almost one million artifacts were dug up and then cataloged in six volumes. The exploration took half a year, and the cataloging another four years. Compare that to Scott and Dan's forty-eight hours.

"Be nice to them," says Maya, Dan's girlfriend, who thinks they are being too harsh on archaeologists. She herself has worked part-time on several official digs.

"This is what you'd call rapid archaeology," Scott says.

Maya gives him a funny look.

"Maybe search-and-destroy," she says, then laughs.

"So what are you saying?" Dan asks, detecting a mocking tone in her voice. "That we're funner?"

"Yeah," she says, arching an eyebrow, "you're funner."

Ironically, it was the ship that Geismar helped exhume in 1981 that focused Scott's attention on digging more seriously and eventually led him to privies. Until then, he and his friend Zach used to pick bottles out of dumps on construction sites, but they had never been diggers. Zach was working in the South Street Seaport area when the ship was discovered, and he heard that it would be open for public viewing for one day only. So among the eleven thousand people who lined up to see it were Scott and Zach, and as they were leaving they noticed that there was a site next door where the archaeologists had finished their exploration and the construction crew had moved in. They decided to start going there late at night, when no one was around, to explore. It was during that time that Scott unearthed the four-thousand-pound cannon and Zach found the item that would become his friend Dave's inspiration, the tricorn Revolutionary hat.

After South Street Seaport, Scott looked for other dig sites. He also hung out at Bottles Unlimited, a unique store on the Upper East Side owned by William "Bottle Bill" Delafield, watching as bottles were bought and sold, and tips were traded. He heard dealers repeatedly talk about pontils, which date back to the mid-nineteenth century and whose name derives from the pontil rod that held them over the fire. A telltale scar would be left on the base of the bottle when it was finally snapped from the rod. One day a man walked into the store with a box of 1850 bottles that he had dug out of a privy in Brooklyn, and after that Scott could think of nothing else besides pontils and privies.

"I wanted to find a pontil. And I was fascinated by the fact that you could dig these old bottles out of a well."

He started searching in the very first place he could think of, his workplace. At the time he was doing odd jobs at an old house in Queens that was owned by a man who was an eccentric and a hoarder. His yard was full of junk that he'd put there or other people had thrown over the fence, and Scott was sure he wouldn't mind him quarrying through the mess.

"He said, 'Go to it. Have fun.'"

After clearing an area of debris, Scott shoveled a trench fifteen feet long, three feet across, and three feet down. Amazingly, one of the first things he found was a pontil, which motivated him more than ever, although he didn't find very much after that. He kept digging in a straight line until the point where his spade hit rock, but instead of going over it, he went around it, eventually uncovering a circle five feet in diameter. When he dug inside the circle, he saw the color and texture of the earth were different. Quite unintentionally, he had found his first privy.

Throughout the morning, Scott and Dan have an audience. The construction workers from the Jane Street house come down in dribs and drabs to smoke cigarettes and watch the men's progress. All of them are Polish immigrants, and their English isn't good, so when Scott and Dan try to explain what they're doing, the men just nod vaguely. Their boss, who speaks some English and is an amateur numismatist, asks them if they ever find coins. Scott gives him an old brass penny they come across, and the man walks away overjoyed.

"At this stage," says Dan, "a penny down a shithole is so corroded, it's not worth anything."

Later on, a man in a suit arrives, someone important from the Jane Street property. He notices the pile that's been gathering slowly on the side of the hole—besides the demijohn, the rubber dog bone, and the breast pump, there are sections of bone and ivory, six toothbrushes, two halves of a pot, bits of porcelain, a ceramic jug. Scott gives him his customary recitation.

The man looks surprised. "This was a toilet?!"

Scott smiles, as if he's never had someone respond this way.

The fact that they've already reached the eight-foot level and nothing substantial has come up yet makes Scott wonder if it's worth going any farther. They suspect that the privy might have been dipped—or cleaned—more carefully than others they've dug in the city.

"At this point," explains Scott, "I do a test hole of two or three feet till I hit the nice soil, which is black as coffee grains, rich and dark brown and black. It's really soft and fluffy and full of window glass, bottles and bones, and shards. Then you know you've got something."

Dan hands down a stick that Scott was sharpening earlier. It looks no more exceptional than a broomstick handle sharpened to a point at one end.

"It's our design," says Scott.

"We invented the sticking process," Dan adds.

Scott is more modest. "Or we *believe* we did."

"Most diggers use a steel claw. They dig through this layer with a shovel, then use a steel claw, and they find that works for them. We use a stick because it's good on your upper body and we can tear right through a layer without hurting anything."

"The claw will rip the lip off a bottle," says Scott, "put a scratch on it. It's really not a good idea."

Scott sticks through a foot of earth, loosening the ground carefully.

"You have to watch out for when it squeaks. Then you know you have hit glass. So you go around it. And we scratch the sides of the well too. There's often stuff lodged there."

Before long, three intact "shitters" (bottles from the 1860s or later) come out. It's a positive sign, so Scott and Dan are more committed to the hole now. As Scott loosens the earth, Dan stands at the top, one hand reaching in front of the other as he pulls up each bucketload of night soil.

Dan is smoother than Scott, taller, darker, more clean-cut, and neater. He's done odd jobs, painted houses, studied Wiccan. For a dozen years he dug bottles along the Hudson River, north of the city. The houses that once stood there were grand, and outside of them were not only privies but also ash heaps, where the residue from the large fireplaces was thrown. The heaps went as deep as eight feet, and things could as easily have been tossed into the ash as into the privies. Dan looked for evidence of both. Many of the houses don't exist anymore, and like the diggers who go in search of destroyed forts in the West, the first thing he must do is figure out where the buildings, ash heaps, and privies might have been.

"It's not easy," he says. "You could walk across them and you wouldn't know it. You get the plans and try to find them, but often new buildings have gone up. Or it's forest. Sometimes there was a slave privy next to the white one. It was always very small." He grunts in disgust. "People couldn't even shit in the same hole."

As Dan pulls up another bucket of soil, his movements are

regular but stiff. Searching for privies has left him with a herniated disk.

"There's no work in this field that isn't extremely arduous. Well diggers, dump diggers, sludgers, metal detectors—it's hard work. You bust your ass doing it."

Scott keeps working throughout the conversation. Kneeling down, he holds the stick like a short oar and picks at the ground, scooping the loosened earth, or fluff, into the bucket. He picks out anything that might have any value or relevance, from a bottle neck to a rat's skull, and puts it in a brown paper bag that he will later hand up to the surface.

You can't see it from the way Scott is bent over, but he resembles a hero out of *The Last of the Mohicans*—long red hair, bushy beard, and a Native American necklace that includes, quite appropriately, a bear's claw. "Roadkill," he says, as much an explanation as a defense.

If his friend Dave's inspiration to hunt for treasure as a boy was a metal detector from RadioShack, Scott's was a place that could easily have sprung from the pages of a tale of lost treasure. Fort Jay, which is on Governors Island, is star-shaped, and parts of it date back to the eighteenth century. Scott lived on the island because his father worked for the Coast Guard. When he was ten, he came across two boys digging in the fort's moat. They showed him what they'd found so far— buttons, coins, and a bottle from 1861—and he was smitten. He asked if he could join them, and by the following day he'd made his own sieve and started digging too. In no time he'd amassed his own collection of buttons from the War of 1812 and the Civil War, coins, pottery shards, and glass beads. When the house across the street from his was being renovated, Scott and a friend went through the excavation, finding a rifle from World War I and a jawbone pierced by a bullet. He arranged many of the discoveries in his window, a precursor to a more spectacular display he would create years later.

Since then, Scott has honed his knowledge, reading about everything he has unearthed. It hasn't been easy. Even archaeologists admit that not much information is available about privies and the way landfill was made in New York, or what went into it. Therefore, Scott has stuck to older books about the city, anything that was written closer to the time in question, as they are likely to be more accurate and more detailed. In their pages he finds what he calls "blips," a line here and a paragraph there, which he puts together to construct a fuller account of the olden days, all of which he relates in the manner of the best raconteur. His diligence is almost teacherlike, and he even takes Dave to task for not being more knowledgeable. When the two of them were working together in Jersey City and Scott found a Brinckerhoffs bottle, Dave couldn't understand his excitement. He'd never heard of a Brinckerhoffs before and was unaware it sold for fifteen hundred dollars.

"Don't you study your manuals?" Scott admonished him, like he might a younger brother. "You should be reading your Greer catalog [an auction listing of some of the most famous medicine bottles] when you're on the toilet."

Whenever Scott sets up at a flea market, his table will be spread with an array of forty or fifty bottles, which might include a Hegeman Co., a Bixby's Shoe Polish, and a brown Watkins Dandruff Remover & Scalp Tonic. Usually he will be talking to someone, explaining that this is a 1910 eyewash or an aqua from Queens, or that he found the 1930s vase on Zeriga Avenue. In one corner he keeps a series of ink bottles— some of them found and obviously old, others brand-new reproductions from China—just to show people the difference. And when you see him deep in conversation, going into detail about the origin of this Eastman or that X. Bazin, it's hard to take the accusation of any peeved archaeologist seriously. If anything, he puts old New York in context, and by digging things up and talking about his finds, he keeps history alive.

"I love bottles," he says, as if there's any doubt. "They're more dramatic, more beautiful, more interesting. Gold doesn't interest me. Some people go down to South America and talk about finding Inca gold. I'd prefer to be digging the seventeenth-century outhouses down there. Now *that's* interesting."

There are enough artifacts laid out in Scott's apartment in Queens to make it seem like a minimuseum. And the view from the living room, quite aptly, is of the place where he's found most of them, Manhattan.

The kitchen is the core of the museum. Forty of Scott's most colorful bottles—aquas, yellows, cobalts, browns, and a single purple—line four shelves across the kitchen window, so that at the right time of day the sun hits them and refracts into the room, transforming the rainbow of rows into a very unusual stained-glass window.

"That purple is the most valuable," Scott says, then explains how at the time of manufacture color often determined rarity. "When they were producing the glass, a factory would get an order for several thousand pieces and do fifty or so with some extra leftover sapphire or topaz glass. Those became the special ones."

All the kitchen walls are also covered in bottles, not mixed, as they are in the window, but organized according to color.

One wall is kept for blues or aquas, which vary in size, depending on whether they are snuffs, mineral waters, or medicines. Other shelves are for browns, either barber bottles or poisons with ribbed or latticed sides in order to make them identifiable by touch in the dark. Around the corner is a medley of greens, from forest green to deep emerald, and one long shelf holds only soda bottles. Down below, under the counter, are bottles for wine, rum, and port, as well as English onion bottles brought from Guyana, Dutch gin bottles, and German mineral bottles.

"These are my real, real bottles," he says of the collection on display, "for looking at every day. Not to ever sell."

Each bottle has a label underneath, explaining where it came from and when. But Scott doesn't need to look at them because he remembers each one's provenance, whether it was from a privy, a construction site, or landfill.

"This is from South Street Seaport," he will say. Or, "I got this from a Chelsea privy, Twenty-first Street." Or, "This is seventeen-nineties, found on Staten Island."

Scott has about five hundred bottles, not including the ones he has planted on the riverbank and in empty lots around the neighborhood. Until recently he had almost double that, but he needed some money and sold off the others.

"I should never have done that," he says remorsefully, sounding as if he had hocked a close relative.

Scott and Dan discover as many as five thousand bottles a year. The shitters they bury, because they don't have anywhere to keep them, but most of the bottles get sold, either to private individuals or at the flea market. The most they have ever gotten for one, which they sold on eBay, was more than three thousand dollars. They usually earn enough from the bottle sales to finance their operation, which costs them about ten

thousand dollars a year. Rarely do they find the really valuable bottles, ones that fetch tens of thousands of dollars, which
usually predate the 1840s.

"Earlier than that, they seem to disappear," Scott says.
"Bottles then were made to keep. Most of the high-end bottles
have been in circulation for years, and they go to auctions.
You don't dig them out the ground now. People have had them
in their houses for a hundred and fifty years, and they are
bought by doctors and lawyers."

Less noticeable in his apartment than the bottles, if only
because they aren't as abundant or displayed as prominently,
are the other items Scott has found at the same sites: Civil
War buttons and badges and bullets, medals, glass syringes, a
cross section of pipe made from pine (the very first water pipes
in Manhattan), slip-decorated pie plates that he has put back
together again (recast and painted so expertly that you can
hardly tell that some of them began as only a few fragments),
stones (all of them from New York parks), shovels, tar buckets,
seals, musket balls.

There are cupboards he has made of found wood and old
hand-wrought nails, one of which is filled with six graphite
crucibles that he pulled out of a derelict glass factory in Jersey
City. Only one of the fragile crucibles is intact, although they
are all so rare that not even the glass museum in upstate New
York has one. As Scott gently retrieves one to show me how
it was used in glassmaking (of course he has read up on the
entire process already), it seems that these objects couldn't
have found a safer or better home.

Anything that is broken or unusable—bits of porcelain,
dolls' heads, warped silver spoons Dave has brought him—
Scott rarely throws away. They end up in brown paper bags,

ensuring that items from a particular site stay together until Scott has a chance to make an artwork out of them. He paints cityscapes on some of the less valuable bottles, and uses the bits of saved artifacts in collages. In the living room is an assortment of collages that he has recently finished. He points out two.

"This one I did from a site in Chinatown—Canal Street near the Brooklyn Bridge. Poor Irish lived there. A lot of clay pipes, beer bottles, and soda bottles. And this one is from pieces of blue delft only."

Each collage has a title on the back. *Three. When the Girl Went Away. Boar's Bite. Mermaid of Time. Loleesha.*

"The name comes to me," Scott says. "Sometimes it takes a while. Like Loleesha. It took about five tries to get it. I would write it and think. It's like she was speaking to me."

The remark sounds a bit dreamy, but the collages fit in perfectly with the assortment of historical America, bears' teeth, old pipes, cannonballs, pie plates, crucibles. The collages are an extension of his bottle museum, pieces of the city's previous life studded in white plaster and stuck on a wall in Queens.

By late afternoon few people bother to come down to see what's happening at the Jane Street dig. They've lost interest. (No gold, no bodies? What's the point?) The excavation, meanwhile, has grown, and you can see how they can get thirty thousand pounds out of one small pit. Piles lie all over the yard—stones here, rocks there, and soil near the fence—divided in a way that makes refilling the hole a lot easier.

The air of expectation has risen in the last hour, for Scott and Dan have found a deep-green soda bottle that leads them to believe they've reached the all-important 1840s layer. Scott, who is down below once again, yells something, but he's too far down to hear clearly. He stands up and shouts the word again.

"Snuff!"

Scott reaches above the rim, and in his hand is a square, dark brown bottle with beveled edges. Why he's excited is that the lip, a wide lip, is intact. The last one that he found totally intact, the *only* other snuff he has dug up intact, was worth fifteen hundred dollars. He gave it to a friend, only to discover its true value later on. As he is brushing off some of the night soil, he notices a crack. It's a small crack, but still, a crack is a crack, which automatically reduces the bottle's price by as much as 70 percent.

"Bottle collectors are as anal as stamp collectors and coin collectors," Scott says.

Dan isn't so sure that Scott will find a buyer at all. Bottles might be the number one small antique in the United States, with prices shooting up to record levels, but buyers are getting pickier than ever. Once again the distinction becomes obvious between themselves and the kind of bottle collectors who don't get their fingernails dirty.

"A collector wouldn't take that," Dave says. "That's the difference between diggers and collectors. We do this to uncover the past. Collectors do it to possess the past."

After the snuff, it's Dan's turn to go down. He won't stay there long, for within ten minutes he unearths an ink. Then, ten minutes after that, Scott finds another snuff. It isn't worth fifteen hundred dollars, but maybe two hundred. Minutes after Dan lets himself down the rope, he finds a second ink, an umbrella ink, so-called because of its shape. It is embossed with something they've never seen before.

"Five hundred dollars!" Scott shouts in excitement, and you can tell he thinks they're on a roll. Dan, ever the pessimist, doesn't seem as sure. A sapphire ink would be worth a lot, but aqua? After he brings it to the surface, he carefully wraps the umbrella ink in paper and puts it in the shade.

"After so many years in the earth, it could crack in the sun. Sometimes you'll be in your house a week after a dig and you'll hear a crack. It'll be one of your bottles."

Dan will probably sell the umbrella ink. He isn't as attached to his bottles as Scott. Even though he has several hundred at his house, he usually keeps only those that have a special meaning to him.

"Scott's collection is much better. I keep the bottles mostly as mementos. Like the one that came from the time a well caved in on me and I almost died."

After the umbrella ink, not much comes up. From the low-key tone of the conversation, you can hear that the dig is drawing to a close. Scott and Dan start taking bets about how many items are still in the hole.

"There's only three more down there," Scott says. "Three bottles, tops."

In fact, they find only two bottles as well as several glazed Chinese marbles, each one worth about thirty dollars. Before they start scooping the piles back into the hole—rocks first, stones second, dirt last—Scott walks off to one side and from out of his bag he retrieves a reproduction historical flask with an eagle embossed on the side. Into it he puts several pennies and quarters, making sure that each one has this year's date. When they are ready, the bottle will be carefully lowered into the well before it is covered and the rest of the excavation is filled up.

"We do this on every hole," says Scott. "It's for anyone who digs here in the future. It is our kind of time capsule."

chapter 9

the preservationist

Every collector has that single item whose importance far outweighs its monetary value. For Dave, it could be the Johnny Ray medallion he gave away at the jazz festival; for Steven, the copy of *Ulysses* with the torn cover; for Nelson, the framed letter signed by John F. Kennedy. For Iver Iversen, it is an oil painting.

The naval scene has never actually been hung on a wall since it was first plucked off a sidewalk, but that was never the intention. It was saved for science, and as a result of tests carried out on it, it resembles a pictorial bar code. The sea changes color from gray to dirty blue to turquoise, while the ship at its center has a clear bow, is foggy amidships, and ends with a poop deck that is hardly visible.

Over a period of years the naval scene has been cleaned up, strip by strip, to show the effectiveness of a machine called the Conservator 2940. The Conservator could very well change the face of art restoration across the globe, opening up the way for artworks centuries old to be returned to their original state. Everything from a small oil to a mural to an expansive cave painting could be seen in the way it was first composed. Until now, the sediment and encrustations that have become attached over the centuries—whether from carbon, candle wax, varnish, or dirt—have for the most part been dislodged with solvents, which have never been a safe medium. Using them poses the danger of taking off too much of the surface. During the restoration of the Sistine Chapel, for instance, areas that Michelangelo had gone over at a later stage with varnish, making small changes, were permanently removed. But by being left untouched, the artworks can suffer another kind of deterioration. The *Mona Lisa* and many other famous paintings were cleaned long ago with an egg-white varnish that has gradually changed the color of the original paint, and until it is removed they will grow yellower and yellower.

Unlike solvents and poultices, the Conservator gets rid of varnish and buildup one layer at a time, and under very controlled conditions—with a laser. Using fiber-optic technology and a handheld control like a pen, the process of removal can be managed more easily, while a foot pedal is manipulated to generate up to fifty thousand pulses a minute.

On the face of it, the Conservator has nothing in common with mongo. Finding the one takes a few hours of physical exertion on any street, doesn't cost a penny, and you don't even have to leave the neighborhood to do it. Designing the Conservator has taken many years of scientific expertise, has cost hundreds of thousands of dollars, and has required extensive travel to all corners of the world. One might as well compare a missile defense system, whose technology the Conservator has utilized, and an unwanted painting of a naval scene that's been tossed out with the garbage. And yet the Conservator probably never would have existed if it weren't for mongo. The connection is Iver Iversen.

In early 1995, Iver received a call from Mary Biddle Semans, the owner of a century-old mansion on Fifth Avenue. Mrs.

Semans was remodeling several rooms, and she wanted to convert two offices back into the reception room that was once there. Visualizing the space she remembered from childhood, Mrs. Semans told Iver about numerous panels painted with colorful scenes of flowers and birds. She suspected that the panels, though they were imported from France in the 1920s, had in fact been made in the eighteenth century. She didn't know who had painted over them, or why, but she wanted to know if the art could be recovered undamaged.

Mrs. Semans called Iver for two reasons. First, he is an expert in historical restoration and has worked on projects as small as a log cabin and as expansive as Plant Hall at the University of Tampa, better known in the early 1900s as the sprawling Moorish-revival Tampa Bay Hotel, where Teddy Roosevelt planned the Spanish Civil War. Second, Iver happens to rent an office on the ground floor of Duke-Semans House.

Iver did several bullets, or test areas, to try and confirm what Mrs. Semans remembered, and in the process he uncovered at least seven coats of latex before reaching the shellac covering the original artwork. Not wanting to risk disturbing the shellac and the potentially valuable art underneath it, he ruled out the use of solvents or poultices. The puzzle of how to expose the mural unscathed began to consume him, not only because Mrs. Semans was a friend he wanted to help but also because he was convinced that he could actually save a 250-year-old work of art. It didn't help that he had to confront the conundrum daily, since the panels were situated on the floor directly above his office.

"That set me off on a quest," he says, "the possibility that we might find a lovely French painting underneath."

Iver contacted two friends, Joe Wiggins and Adele Decruz,

a physicist and an inventor at Duke University, who both had worked in laser research. One of them had met a Russian scientist several years earlier, and he had mentioned that there was an experimental model of a hydrogen chloride laser at the Efremov Scientific Research Institute of Electrophysical Apparatus in St. Petersburg. The laser had originally been created as an antimissile defense system during the Star Wars arms buildup but had never been used for that purpose. With a wavelength almost double that of any other laser in the world, it sounded perfect for the trio's needs. They made contact with Efremov and were allowed to take several paintings to St. Petersburg for testing.

The outcome was better than they had hoped for, but a major problem remained: the size of the machine, which had mirrors and arms that would have better suited a dental surgery. The model at Efremov was as big as a tabletop and could never be taken onto scaffolding or into the armpit of a statue to do the sensitive, intricate work required. The Americans believed that they could create something smaller by using fiber optics. At the same time, they began testing another kind of laser, one that would prove even more effective than hydrogen chloride. At its core was an iridium crystal.

After seven more years, a fortune in research and development money, numerous revisions in order to comply with European Union regulations, and countless trips across the United States, as well as to St. Petersburg and Florence, the Conservator has gone through several generations. Though manufactured by Schwartz Electro-Optics in Florida, research has been taken over by the Italian government through a laboratory in Florence. The Italian interest in the machine is understandable, for it might hold the best solution yet to repairing countless paintings that were coated in polyurethane as a protective measure after the 1967 floods in Florence and, as a result, have gone gray between the surfaces. So much faith has been placed in the Conservator that it has already been used on a Titian, a Caravaggio, the *Gates of Paradise* at the Duomo, and Giotto's *Crucifix*. Before them all, though, it was tested on a naval scene plucked out of the garbage on the Upper East Side of New York.

The panels in Mrs. Semans's reception room, the catalyst for the laser, weren't mongo, but they easily could have been. The intention behind unmasking them was the same as for picking something off of the street: Iver wanted to save them from oblivion. The act of a historical preservationist was, in this case, not very different from that of a street collector.

Iver Iversen, it so happens, is both, and the union of profession and pastime couldn't have been more serendipitous. For Iver has an ability that is uncanny even among mongo collectors to identify a rarity lying on the sidewalk or in a Dumpster, no matter how damaged or forlorn it may be. He can tell the origin and monetary value of something that less scrupulous collectors would pass up because (1) it doesn't look like it would be worth the trouble of taking home and then repairing, (2) it is only one part of a much bigger puzzle that they don't have the knowledge or patience to solve, or (3) they don't think it has any value at all. Sometimes the item doesn't look like anything at all, simply a piece of scrap. But Iver can imagine it as it once was and, if he has anything to do with it, it will be again—not on a dump but restored to its former glory and placed on a mantel or added to the décor of some magnificent atelier.

Iver has been honing his craft since he attended Tulane University in New Orleans in the 1970s. He was already a collector by then, having started as a boy on a farm in Iowa, where he watched his father gather old pieces of steel from the dump to use at home or take a fridge handle to replace their own. "My father learned from his father, and he from his, all the way back to the old country." As a student, Iver picked up furniture or used found objects to make a study carrel in his bedroom or a bar in the communal room. He was also profoundly affected by a practice that was taking root in New Orleans at the time, the reuse and rehabilitation of old or damaged décor and furniture. People would remove nineteenth-century ceilings and parquet floors from houses about to be demolished to install elsewhere, while there were several shops on Magazine Street that made reproduction parts for imperfect objects. A one-knobbed door or a three-legged chair could have their missing pieces recast quite inexpensively.

"Not many places in the country were thinking along those lines back then," Iver says. The impact this restoration movement had on him clearly influenced his work and his collecting from then on, to the benefit of both. "I left New Orleans with a thorough understanding of the styles and the different periods [of interiors] and a knowledge that a person could make money from doing these things."

Today Iver will walk down a street and see not a dirty chest of drawers on the sidewalk but a nineteenth-century mahogany dresser that, with six hundred dollars' worth of work, could be worth triple that amount. A series of metal-and-glass skeletons in a Dumpster aren't just some broken light fittings but three art deco lamps that can be reworked and rebrassed and their parts interchanged at a cost of about one thousand dollars to create a pair that in a store would sell for six thousand.

Unfortunately for Iver—or maybe fortunately, considering his views on preservation—he doesn't stumble across damaged art deco lamps and scratched nineteenth-century dressers every day of the week. But wood he does find, and its widespread availability is one of the reasons why he can often be seen dragging lumber across the city late at night.

"I go for woods a lot because I know them and they're easy to transform into something else," he says. (In Plant Hall, whose passageways were the longest in the western hemisphere before the Pentagon was built, Iver was responsible for the restoration of the wood.)

Whereas most people might see a piece of wood in a Dumpster and think it's a useless floorboard or a splintered rafter discarded from a gutted apartment, Iver sees opportunity. And unlike Billy Jarecki or Jeffrey, who would have created something new and different, Iver uses it to restore something old or make something that could pass for old. A fragment of century-old cherry or irreplaceable walnut might be shaved down, cut, and reworked into a similarly dated sash window or door frame.

Right outside Iver's office in Duke-Semans House is a good example of this kind of restoration. The wood trim in the hallway had been modernized over the years, painted black, with random bits of plywood added here and there, an obvious patch-up job. Constantly faced with this unsightly clash of materials, Iver wanted to find something that matched the original white oak door leading to the street, even though he knew it would be difficult to find. White oak, which has a distinctive tiger stripe in it, has been virtually impossible to obtain since the 1920s.

"You find all kinds of red oak, but not white oak with its beautiful form."

But Iver is persistent, and he kept going through Dumpsters for several months until he found what he was looking for. In a Dumpster not far from his apartment, buried deep under the debris from a renovation job, were several window frames, all of them white oak. He retrieved more than enough wood to redo all the trim in the hallway.

Whenever Iver is out on the street, he not only spots rare items—the long-gone woods, the vitrine that's missing a leg, the century-old paneling ripped from a wall—but he is also thinking about where they might go and who might need them. In many cases, he is able to find a home for them.

"I do it as a hobby primarily," he says. "People know me to have a clever sense of design. They'll be in a new condo, and it's just very bland and awful, and they'll want the fireplace to jump out. They'll ask me what to do, and oftentimes I'll land up shipping them pieces I have found."

Around the corner from Duke-Semans House, Iver came across more than a thousand used bricks, double-fired and obviously part of an interior wall that had been removed from another mansion. It took several trips, but he got them loaded into trash cans, put onto dollies, and wheeled back to Fifth Avenue. The bricks were eventually used to build an entire interior wall, which included a large fireplace.

"There's a certain joy to using stuff that's been thrown away," Iver says. "It's very satisfying knowing that it is no longer going out to [a dumpsite on] Staten Island. I am pretty up-front with people about using found stuff, and they're usually amused by it. Sometimes they're downright jealous."

When the billionaire industrialist David Koch bought Jackie Onassis's apartment after she died, Iver kept an eye on what was tossed out during the renovation. His office being only a few streets away, he passed the building every day, hoping to find something he could use. And eventually he did. Protruding from a Dumpster was a cream-colored pantry door with a panel of frosted glass at eye level. Iver had been wanting to replace the bathroom door in his own apartment, so that's exactly where the former first lady's pantry door went.

"At the time all these people were spending a fortune getting something of Jackie O's at Sotheby's—a lot of it trash—and I picked up her door for nothing. I love telling people that. They think it's so cool. It was also a good object lesson."

Anyone who finds out about the Jackie Onassis door might pass a Dumpster afterward and look twice, but very few people would be able to discern the remnants of, say, a mahogany staircase or a Gothic room. And, as Iver points out, Gothic rooms land up in Dumpsters a lot more often than he'd care to know about.

Gothic rooms were all the rage at the turn of the twentieth century, when Duke-Semans House was only one of the many mansions being built in upper Manhattan. Fifth Avenue alone saw replicas of French châteaux and Renaissance palazzi erected for the likes of Payne Whitney, the Vanderbilts, Henry Frick, and Andrew Carnegie, who decorated them with a fantastic array of antiques, paintings, and entire rooms that had been imported from Europe and Asia. The home of Otto Kahn, a millionaire and philanthropist, featured not only a Gothic room, but an Italian room, a Louis Quinze sitting room, an Italian Renaissance Revival staircase, the paneling and fixtures for which were all imported from France. When William Randolph Hearst moved into his five-floor apartment at the Clarendon, on Riverside Drive, his almost acre-size apartment included a Gothic room, as well as English, Greek, and Julius Caesar rooms, while the elevator was created out of a confession box from the Vatican. The Hearst residence was gutted in 1940, when the building was taken over by an insurance company, and the only reason Iver wasn't furious about that particular gut job was he hadn't been born yet.

In Iver's attempts to find a home for what he finds, the most receptive destination has turned out to be his landlord's Duke-Semans House. Not only did Mrs. Semans ask his advice about the dining room panels, indirectly inspiring the Conservator, but her son also encouraged Iver to install found objects wherever possible. For it turns out that James Semans also has a taste for mongo.

"Despite being fourth-generation money," says Iver, "he has a basement full of found things."

Consequently, almost every floor of the seven-story mansion has been turned into a showcase of rescued objects, from door plates to wall units, from floors to ceiling beams, from tiles to toilets. It was here that the thousand bricks taken from around the corner were used to make a wall and fireplace. When James wanted to alter the bathroom on the first floor, he asked Iver if he would do it using as much as possible from the street. An added request was that it should resemble "something out of the *Orient Express*."

What Iver created might be too big for a train, but the ambience is appropriately 1920s: a marble sink from which the paint had to be scraped and, supporting it, a bronze pedestal with a gargoyle, which came from a city marquee; two different types of marble tile, some from an old laundry and others from an office block; subway tiles taken from a Dumpster; two large slabs of marble in the shower that were rejected from a construction site for being too sugary; an incandescent Lumaline light fixture; and a toilet from around the corner. Only the ceiling was new.

In the apartments upstairs, one of which takes up two floors and the other five, the mongo is more expansive. The wall of bricks, which went into the smaller apartment, was so long and high that it could comfortably accommodate not only a fireplace but also a mahogany door, a metal fire door, and several oak panels, all of them rescued. Small by comparison, but a special favorite of Iver's nevertheless, is a strangely colored door that serves as an entryway to the firewood storage area. The white pine it's made of was so old by the time it was found and sanded down that it had turned as orange as a pumpkin.

On the topmost story, almost one hundred square feet of floor had to be added after alterations were completed. Once again the right wood for the job wasn't readily available, cyprus in this case, but Iver came up with exactly the type and quantity he needed. After scouring numerous Dumpsters, he found a supply in two different locations, and it was then reworked into tongue-and-groove pallets.

There is a found object in practically every room of the mansion. Metal cabinets from the street were sanded down and installed in one of the kitchens. A series of twelve-foot-long, four-inch I beams tossed out of a building in Harlem were used to support a cracked bedroom ceiling. A 150-pound shower door made in the 1950s, solid brass with chrome overlay and a beautiful glass panel, was considered so exquisite that a shower stall was specially built to accommodate it. Two bathtubs were taken from the sidewalk not only because they were in good condition but also because of their unusual design—they were cast at an angle, so that anyone lying in them would face not toward the faucets and the opposite wall, but outward, into the bathroom.

What Iver prizes most of all, though, is not what you'd expect, not the twenty-foot walls built of found bricks or the art deco lamps that were reworked into six-thousand-dollar spectacles, but the out-of-date minutia that he finds a new, old-looking purpose for, or the replacement piece that fits in so snugly you'd think it had always been there. During one of the renovation projects at Duke-Semans House, two workers on their lunch break were walking around the neighborhood when they came upon an old cast-iron-and-glass door, the flap-open kind that used to be a commonplace feature in the sidewalks outside shops in lower Manhattan.

"As soon as they saw it, they knew it was something I'd love," says Iver. "So they brought it back to the house. And we designed it right in."

A step was needed to go from the hallway into one of the kitchens, so instead of making it out of brick, wood, or metal, Iver utilized the glass-dotted door and lit it from underneath. He clearly loves the fact that an article someone else had deemed useless had, on being saved, regained not one function but two: as a step and as a source of illumination.

"So you don't have to turn on the ceiling lights if you want to raid the fridge at night."

The detail that has given Iver the most pleasure, however,

is the brass plate under an unusually large doorknob. The plate had been severely damaged, and Iver couldn't find a replacement part anywhere. The early-twentieth-century hardware hadn't been produced for a long time, and Iver had even, as a last resort, scoured salvage stores for a replica. Walking his dogs late one night, he saw a door with exactly the right size plate leaning against the garbage of an apartment building. But it was so filthy that he first went home to change, then returned in old clothes and armed with a flashlight and a screwdriver.

"While I was unscrewing the plate," he says, "the doorman of the building came out. He saw my nasty clothes and said something to me, and I just mumbled an answer like a homeless person."

Iver doesn't know what possessed him to put on an act, and he was just as surprised by the doorman's response. The man gave him a few dollars and asked him not to make a mess. When Iver got the doorplate back to the mansion, he was thrilled to find he'd guessed correctly. It was just the right size.

Much like the doorplate, everything that has been added to Duke-Semans House fits perfectly. The last thing that crosses your mind when walking around the Fifth Avenue mansion today is that some or other fixture amid all the Old World magnificence had a previous life on a modern-day street. Even Iver sometimes has trouble identifying what was found and what wasn't, for he wasn't the only person to introduce rescued objects. The interior decorator who came in after him did too. She didn't get them off the street, though, but bought them from Irreplaceable Artifacts, a very costly salvage store. Iver smiles at the irony.

"She did in a very expensive way what I did in a very inexpensive way."

What is mongo in Iver's own home is more noticeable than in Duke-Semans House, but that's because his apartment is less of a destination for the pieces he finds than a way station. Some fit in, while others look as though they are being made to fit in until a better place can be found.

Most of what is inside the tenth-floor penthouse Iver keeps, what is outside he doesn't. Besides the Jackie Onassis pantry door, there are Baedeker travel guides from the early 1900s in the bookshelf, a headboard in the main bedroom, a painting of a woman Iver tells everyone is his mother, a wall of glass bricks used to make a bathroom, doors transformed into bunk beds, old Louis Vuitton trunks piled in a corner of Iver's study, as well as a stray dog Iver picked up off a beach in Mexico.

On the wide L-shaped terrace are the objects whose fate is still undecided. In between a jungle of plants lie numerous pieces of terra-cotta, obtained from a building on Central Park West that Iver collected at, off and on, for an entire summer. Like many wealthy prewar buildings, it was replacing its terra-cotta with limestone, the material it was once meant to resemble. A mahogany door is being left out until the rain loosens the paint, for, as Iver points out, New York's rigorous repainting laws have resulted in this kind of 1930s door having as many as thirty coats of paint. Farther along the terrace are enough subway tiles to do the walls of two bathrooms and a kitchen, all gathered from a building belonging to the Iranian government. Iver went back night after night to pick through the tiles, which were torn out during a renovation, and came home each time with several buckets filled to the brim. His means of transportation, as always, was one of three dollies that he keeps for his nocturnal forays.

"As long as I can get something onto a dolly, I can get it home," he says. "I don't mind pulling it ten or twenty blocks. I'll find some crackhead and give him ten bucks to help me. Sometimes it takes me several hours."

One night Iver and his wife, Rose, were heading home from a restaurant when he saw three slabs of windowsill, each weighing several hundred pounds, on the edge of the sidewalk. They were half a mile from home, but Iver fetched a dolly and wheeled the slabs back to the apartment one by one. They were eventually used as lintels on the radiators.

"Rose just goes nuts sometimes," he says, recalling the occasion they were on their way to a black-tie dinner when he saw a Dumpster and stopped to climb in. He got so dirty that he had to go home and change. "She will see a Dumpster ahead and suddenly will want to take a left because she knows that I can't stand not to look in. But by the same token, I'll get a call from her sometimes and she'll say, 'You've got to get over here!'"

The night Iver found the mahogany doors, though, he was out not with his wife but walking the dogs. It's the perfect time for mongo snooping, as many a collector with a dog will tell you, for a dog takes its time and often leads you down a road you might not have taken. And discovering mongo, as collectors will also confess, is as much about luck as coincidence.

During their walk that night, they passed the Otto Kahn mansion, opposite the Cooper-Hewitt Museum. Kahn's Italianate palazzo, which was one of the largest private houses ever built in Manhattan and once contained artwork by

Botticelli, Rembrandt, and Frans Hals, was being renovated into a school for girls, the Convent of the Sacred Heart. As Iver turned the corner that the mansion is on, he saw that the garbage had already been put out and a man was going through it.

"He got very territorial when he saw me showing an interest."

But he was a black-bag guy, and Iver was after something else altogether. His attention was immediately drawn to several large pieces of wood that turned out to be two sets of mahogany doors. Iver was so preoccupied with figuring out how to get them home, he didn't even notice that the keyholes were covered with large doorplates. When he later cleaned one of them (with the Conservator, naturally), he discovered that it was decorated with a Greek head and had gold chasing underneath that was so beautiful it could have been an article of jewelry. What he at first thought was gold plating turned out to be fifteen-carat gold.

Equally incredible was that all four doors had been hacked in half. As Iver headed home to offload the dogs and get his station wagon to pick up the doors, he knew that even if they were glued and pinned together they would remain scarred.

"I got so angry," he says. "You couldn't get this kind of mahogany again. These trees are long gone. They grew for how many centuries, got cut down by some mogul who had doors made out of them, used them for fifty years, and then they got thrown in the attic. Now some idiot, instead of calling people who would gladly pay for the doors, cut them in half in order to take them out to the street. There was blood over one of them, so he had obviously hurt himself doing it."

For Iver, the act of collecting is more about preserving than

about getting something off the sidewalk for free. As far as
Otto Kahn's doors go, he had arrived in time to collect them
but too late to preserve them intact. Iver, in that sense, is a
Superman of salvage. And if he can't be everywhere at once,
keeping an eye out for anything that's on the verge of being
destroyed, then he pays others to do it for him. On construction sites, he regularly gets whoever on the team is in charge
of filling the Dumpster to put things aside for him and then
he comes by to collect them at the end of the day. He has
friends around the city who call him up when they notice
something that might be of interest.

Even when Iver is traveling, he is on the lookout, and nothing
stands in the way of his bringing things back with him, not
their size, weight, or provenance. From Napa, California, he
brought back a pilot's cabin; from a street in Iowa City, a
cast-iron Chambers gas stove; from a house on the Mississippi,
extensive carvings made by a Swedish immigrant; from a sidewalk near his apartment, a turn-of-the-century cast-iron water
heater; and from a back street in Florence, Italy, four pairs of
peeling green wooden shutters.

Each find has had a different fate, which shows that even
though Iver might have the best intentions for it, a home
doesn't always present itself quickly, if ever. The pilot's cabin,
for instance, became the paneling in a friend's bedroom. The
Italian shutters were hauled to the nearest corner and trans-
ported by cab back to his hotel, where a fellow American
bought them from him and had them shipped back to the
United States. The carvings by the Swede, which celebrate the
flora and fauna of America, Iver has kept. (They have a special
significance, for he himself is the descendent of Scandinavian
immigrants to the Midwest.) The water heater, completely lined

with copper, was so huge that a welder had to come and cut it into three pieces, the heaviest of which weighed twelve hundred pounds.

Iver thinks that the base of the water heater will one day make a great freestanding shower in a loft, but in the meantime it lies, along with most of the carvings and the stove, as well as plenty of other objects, in two thirty-foot storage units he keeps for this purpose. They are out of sight maybe, but hardly ever out of mind and, most important, saved.

But Iver can save only so much. In his professional life, he tries to prevent destruction before it can take place, especially by testifying in court cases about construction law. And he has his foot soldiers out there scouting for him on the streets of New York. But as a member of the public, all he can do is rant and fulminate against ignorance, oversight, and bad taste, which he does regularly. At the receiving end of his tirades is anyone who is in a position to decide the fate of an interior: gung-ho superintendents of buildings, incautious contractors, and thoughtless decorators, the very same ones, I would guess, whom Steven accuses of throwing out the old books with the old décor.

"Ignorance really annoys me," Iver says. "I think decorators know fireplaces and aren't so quick to throw out, say, a French fireplace. But they're not so adept at flooring or ceilings. They will come in and say, 'Out it goes.' They'll make the place all white and stainless steel and ever so chichi. Which is fine. But you don't destroy something that's at least two centuries old in the process. On construction sites, pieces only become valuable once the workers see someone wants them. A lot of great stuff gets wiped out, and that to me is shameful." He shakes his head. "If I could only catch it before it happened."

In Iver's eyes, one of two paths can be taken. His way, where careful attention is paid to the history of a building, what gets taken out and what it gets replaced with, and the wrong way. A building in New York that has followed the correct course, he believes, is the National Arts Club, its Gothic façade a well-known sight on the southern side of Gramercy Park. And a building that hasn't? Well, there are plenty. The foyer of the Chrysler Building, the AMC Empire multiplex on Forty-second Street, and, most noticeably, the National Academy of Science.

Built in 1919, the neo-Italianate Renaissance palazzo was previously the home of Norman Bailey Woolworth. There are still original features, such as a sixteenth-century mantel in the entrance hall and walls of English oak in the library, but modern fittings from discount hardware chains have been added at random.

"Anyone with an eye can walk through that building and pick out every piece that has been replaced, and the rest of it has been trashed," says Iver. As always, he makes the slap-dash mix of valuable-old and discount-new sound like a crime. "A fabulous old wall sconce becomes garbage. They don't have a building supervisor who knows what he's doing. So some junior makes these decisions."

As many of the city's mansions become schools, museums, and other publicly used facilties, the Gothic rooms are only the first of many spaces that get altered. Often much is done correctly, especially on larger projects, but the detail doesn't get the same attention. And if you want to see Iver hit the roof, show him a 1920s light fixture that's been replaced with a $9.95 special from the hardware store.

"I'm talking about the little day-to-day things. I can't begin to fight that. You can't go to the president of the organization and say, 'What kind of idiot does this!' And it happens all the time. For a building to lose what was acquired and put into the original design, to not repair plumbing fixtures and panels and so on, and to just get the cheapest thing doesn't make any sense to me."

This creeping home improvement culture, which makes it so easy to drive down to the mall and buy a replacement fitting that you wouldn't think to try to preserve what you have, is iniquitous to Iver. He also knows why it happens—fixing an old door and bringing it back to its original condition might cost two thousand dollars, while a new door costs six hundred—even though that doesn't make it easier to accept.

"You can't walk down any block of New York and not see one of those Home Depot–style doors with a shiny brass handle and horrible smoked glass, something that looks retro to the eighties, in a golden oak finish. Which might be appropriate in California, but not here."

Wayne Urffer, a schoolteacher in southern New Jersey, could be a pupil of Iver's. He began collecting when he lived in a working-class suburb of old row houses in Philadelphia and saw Dumpsters full of paneled doors with their brass and porcelain hardware intact. Since then he has saved double-hung sash windows, century-old timber, and furniture, although he remembers one 1940s oak end table in particular that put his collecting in perspective.

"It was sitting on the sidewalk right next to the empty Ikea box that had held its replacement. Now, lots of Ikea furniture is perfectly attractive—I've even salvaged a piece or two over the years—but do you think that Ikea end table will still be in use sixty years from now?"

Occasionally, Iver comes across the act of ignorance at the very moment it's being perpetrated. Rollerblading down Central Park West one afternoon, he passed the Beresford, the ornate apartment building where celebrities like Jerry Seinfeld live. A maintenance man was hacking up some wood, and when Iver saw exactly what kind of wood it was, he felt a chill pass through him. It was the paneling from an eighteenth-century library.

"Somebody fifty years ago brought it from Europe and had it installed into a tiny little room. Now some friggin' decorator decided they didn't like it or whatever, and they were going to make it an end to the living room. People don't like small libraries anymore, so they just chucked it. They didn't know what they had. It was clearly boiserie from the seventeen-hundreds. You didn't have to be a genius to know that."

Iver still cringes at the memory of what he did next.

"It's the angriest I've ever been. I was standing on the street, screaming at this poor guy that what he was doing was worse than child abuse. And I thought as the words were coming out, 'Oh, my God, I've got to get out of here.'"

It isn't often that an incident leaves Iver hopeful, or convinced that he has made a convert, but it happens. Several times a year he rents a truck to scour Harlem, where entire blocks are in the process of being gentrified, and contractors often throw out everything that looks a bit tired. Like Wayne Urffer's neighbors who were renovating in Philadelphia and throwing out century-old doors to bring in hollow wood ones, they were "upgrading."

"There are places where they do a gut renovation of a building and they will pull out all the old doors," says Iver. "On Hamilton Terrace, I've found whole Dumpsters full of doors. People are not very clever when they remodel these places. If you go to other parts of the world, they are so much cleverer about reusing things. With us Americans, everything has to be new. It's cheaper, but in the long run there's so much quality that's being trashed. People don't know what they have."

On St. Nicholas Avenue, Iver came across a Dumpster containing a stained-glass window from an 1890s brownstone. Still in its frame and standing about two feet by four, it was stuck in a corner, with objects propped up against it. Iver, as is his custom, went to the nearest park, St. Nicholas in this case, and gave a homeless guy ten dollars to help him. They worked for several hours repacking things and finally got the window out.

When Iver returned a few days later, he heard that he had missed two more windows buried farther down. A man in a nearby house, who had been watching Iver and the homeless man, had come down when they left and dug through the Dumpster on his own. At the very bottom he found the two windows.

"I didn't get them, but now they're being enjoyed some-where," says Iver. "It's great that I inspired him to do that."

Today the stained-glass window is in Iver's office. So are Otto Kahn's doors, nailed and glued together, and fitted perfectly into a ten-foot alcove, one door handle gleaming gold, the other purposely left as Iver found it. They are exam-ples of what was and what could be again.

On the floor near one of the doors is the bar code naval scene, although it doesn't get taken out to do tests on anymore.

The Conservator has been so fully taken over by the Florentines that Iver hardly ever has anything to do with it. Which is why when he and one of its inventors, Adele Decruz, found out that an art preservationist from Florence was going to be giving a lecture at New York University, they decided to go hear what she had to say.

The Italian was in the United States, in fact, to encourage fine-art students to come do their postgraduate work in Italy. Much of her talk focused on how exciting the field was now, especially because of a discovery that could change the face of art restoration. She was, of course, talking about the laser.

"It really gave us a kick sitting in the audience—she didn't know we were there—and hearing about the Conservator spoken of like that."

The lecturer probably wouldn't have believed Iver if he'd told her that it had all started with the panels in Mrs. Semans's house, panels that, ironically, were one of the few things that he never managed to save. That's because they didn't exist, at least not as she remembered. When Iver finally took down a corner panel to examine the back, he discovered that they weren't eighteenth century at all. The paintings of birds and flowers that Mrs. Semans recalled had, in fact, been in another house. The panels above Iver's office were eventually stripped down to the bare wood.

chapter 10

the cowboy

When Iver goes out at night, he sometimes sees Charles, who lives down the street from him. "Now there's a collector," Iver tells me. "You won't believe what he has found."

It isn't the first time that one collector leads me to another, if I haven't already found them through means of my own. Often they don't see each other for a long time, or their collecting lives crossed only very briefly, but they remember each other for years afterward. Scott met Jeffrey when he knocked on the door of 143 Allen Street hoping to dig up the yard. Dave used to hang out at Bottles Unlimited with Scott. Steven regularly bumps into Christiana, who, as a result, has started collecting books too. Steven also knows Eddie the Soda Can King and dozens of other canners, who, he is wont to say, are his colleagues. These collectors can't be called a network, but no matter how different their collections, they all know where the other's mongo comes from and they all believe, as the linen woman at the Twenty-sixth Street flea market put it, that the street is best.

The morning I meet Iver's neighbor Charles, he is standing in front of the refectory of St. Patrick's Cathedral, pondering which fragment he'd take home with him if he got the chance. The spire, he decides. Well, maybe also a cornice or two. Actually, the doors aren't bad either. "Yes, the doors. They blow me away." After he considers the nineteenth-century Catholic church on Madison Avenue for a little longer, the arches, the arcades, the thick supporting walls, he wonders why he's bothering to go small. He might as well take the whole roof, stone vaulting and all.

"But then again," he says, thinking aloud, "you'd have to get it down intact." Even though he has witnessed enough roofs coming down to know the amount of work it takes, he's never had to tackle the job by himself. "You'd have to rely on the guys tearing up the place to get it down for you."

There isn't the slightest chance that St. Patrick's Cathedral or the refectory will be demolished anytime soon. Indeed, as Charles himself admits, the city's old buildings are now less likely than ever to see a wrecking ball. But this doesn't stop us from speculating, and for Charles it's like being a child in a candy store. A steeple or a capital? A column or a statue? In the end, he can't decide what he'd like most, but he knows one thing for sure: Much as he'd hate it if they were ever to knock down either building, he'd be there to pick up the pieces. He has been there numerous times before.

Charles collects New York's unwanted buildings. Or rather, he collects bits of them. Mostly he goes for something smaller than a roof, but usually it is large enough to require plenty of muscle power to get it into the back of his truck. So before he heads to a demolition site he makes a detour to pick up a few helpers, usually at the youth hostel on Amsterdam Avenue, near where he lives. Sometimes, when there's a heavier object—a pillar, a statue, a cornerstone—he also needs a crane.

"It costs a lot, but it's the only way to do it," he says. "It comes with the territory." The inherent difficulty in collecting chunks of buildings is, and always has been, outweighed by Charles's deep respect for what they represent. "A stone is a solid piece. You're not going to take a bat and break it. And if it's carved, you've got a serious piece of work. It has an essence. And it controls space."

Charles calls the pieces of buildings he has accumulated "stones." "My stones," he says. He also talks about them as if they were alive. "The stones argue for their space," he says. "The stones need to be heard."

Even though his collection extends to much more than just chunks of marble, granite, sandstone, and flint—he also has dozens of old mahogany railway ties, many yards of metal fencing, wooden sculptures—it's the stones that mean the most to him.

"They represent an era," he says. "They represent architecture that's irreplaceable."

Ironically, for a collection that is today so enormous, Charles began with something relatively small, which he got from a not particularly memorable building far away from New York. Back in the 1970s, as an art student in Palm Beach, Florida, he had been asked to sketch a house that was being torn down.

"My teacher, Mr. Archer, sent me out to draw this place one of his former pupils was demolishing. When I got there and saw what they were taking out, I said, 'How can you do this?' I still have the doors from that building."

Charles left home that morning an artist and came back that night a collector, the course of his life inarguably changed. From another demolition he took a stone fireplace, and from yet another, several iron gates. Everything went into the garden behind the bungalow where he was living at the time. Gradually he also started lining the property with pieces of concrete, for whenever Charles came across a sidewalk being ripped up he took the slabs home for paving. What he created was less a landscaped garden than an installation of mongo. It also turned out to be a miniature version of something much grander that he would assemble in New York in the years to come.

"I wanted to make something so beautiful that I wouldn't want to leave Florida and go back to New York," he says, but in the end it didn't have the desired effect. Charles returned to Manhattan, in part because he wanted to carry on his art studies at Pratt, but also in part because a certain building there had caught his fancy.

During a previous visit to the city, Charles's car had broken down on Central Park West and 106th Street. He approached a woman raking leaves outside a nearby building, and they started talking. Her name was Marie Drew, and behind her was a grand building, a faux château dating back to the 1880s built of red bricks and sandstone, though its most imposing features were five squat towers with conical roofs. Once the country's first cancer hospital, it had later become the Towers Nursing Home, before closing its doors under a cloud of mismanagement. It wasn't clear how Marie Drew managed to live there, but she did.

The way buildings figure in Charles's life, there was something serendipitous about his vehicle breaking down outside such a notable structure. To him it looked like a castle, and after he paid Marie Drew a second visit, she asked if he wanted to rent a studio there. It didn't bother him that the building was in a poor state of repair, there was no water or electricity, or that his bed was a stretcher in the old nurses' quarters. He was smitten by the idea of living inside a piece of historical New York.

"And that was one of the reasons I came back."

It wasn't the first time that Charles would move into a New York address that was well-known, if not for its architecture then for its bizarre design or the lore surrounding it. Before leaving for Palm Beach, he had lived for a year at the twelve-story Chelsea Hotel on Twenty-third Street, which was built around the same time as the Towers Nursing Home and had, at various stages, accommodated O. Henry, Mark Twain, Bette Davis, and Andy Warhol, who shot *The Chelsea Girls* there.

But at the faux château a new dimension was added to Charles's love of gorgeous old buildings. For the first time in New York he started collecting them. Since then he has become the owner of discarded pieces of Columbia University (two granite columns, nine metal fences and gates); the Cathedral of St. John the Divine (an altar carved with a Star of David); St. Alphonso's Church on West Broadway, which was knocked down to make way for the SoHo Grand Hotel (a granite lion, a stone with an all-seeing eye, a crucifix); P.S. 64 in East New York (two capitals, two cornerstones); and Mt. Sinai Hospital (three capitals). From the Towers Nursing Home he didn't get any stones—even though it was dilapidated, it wasn't being demolished—but when he finally left he made sure to take as many old door handles as he could unscrew. The building was about to be auctioned off, so he was sure the doors would be trashed anyway.

If pressed to identify his best stones, Charles would go with the ones from Mt. Sinai. In 1986, the hospital knocked down ten interconnecting buildings on Fifth Avenue, all of them dating back to 1904, in order to make way for the glass-roofed, pyramidlike Guggenheim Pavilion designed by I. M. Pei. As Charles had done at several demolitions since his Palm

Beach days, he went there intending to draw the buildings as they came down.

"They demolished them quickly. They had to, because it was a landmark. They found all kinds of things in the cornerstone—gold coins, a bottle of wine, newspapers, like a time capsule."

Whether or not it was because he personally watched the Mt. Sinai structures come down piece by piece, Charles is almost reverential when he talks about this particular demolition, saying, "What they tore down was a holy kingdom."

A man on the crew recognized Charles from a previous demolition job, where they'd even helped him load some granite columns onto his truck. When he saw Charles at Mt Sinai, he told him to take whatever he wanted, and he and his men not only helped Charles load them up, but they also put aside fragments of the hospital for him to collect later on. These included a section of stone with the words MT. SINAI carved in it and three of the seven capitals holding up the gigantic granite A-frame that dominated the main building. Each capital was as big as the front end of a car.

"Other people would offer the construction guys money for the stones," Charles says, "but they knew those guys would sell them down the road. They liked me because they knew I was going to keep them."

Every collector has at least one helper. It could be someone at the take-out place who leaves the leftover sushi on top of the garbage bag, the maintenance guys who put aside bags for the canners, the policeman who turns a blind eye to Scott and Dave collecting on a construction site in New Jersey, the demolition team that helps Charles. They are the opposite of the doormen who cut the cords on TVs and douse books with water, and even if they aren't collectors themselves they are standing on the sideline rooting for them.

At the time of the Mt Sinai demolition, Charles had already left the Towers Nursing Home and was living in an unused building in Bedford-Stuyvesant that used to be the Prudential Bank. His arrangement with the landlord was a favorable one, even in the 1980s. All he had to pay was the property taxes, which amounted to less than a thousand dollars a year. The bank was at least a century old, and even though it wasn't famous, there was a vague tie to a New York building that was. And to Charles, that made a difference.

"The owner was Cecil Bowen. I called him Mr. B. He also had the Brooklyn Apollo Theater, which was just like the Apollo in Harlem."

Next door to the bank was a yard where Charles put the capitals from Mt. Sinai and all the pieces he'd brought back from Florida, including an industrial ceramic potbellied stove and some sliding doors, as well as what he had gathered so far in New York. Along one side of the bank he built a wall from dozens of mahogany ties that he'd acquired when the railroad mechanisms were changed.

The bank in Bedford-Stuyvesant was the third location in the city Charles had for his stones. Before that, when he was living in a loft in Ashland Place, near the Brooklyn Academy of Music, he was allowed to put them in a yard next to his building. Luckily for him when he moved there, a construction crew working at BAM helped him move them with their backhoe.

Both the BAM and Bedford-Stuyvesant properties were perfect for the stones—spacious and cheap—but neither could compare to their very first home in New York, which was centrally located, had a crane, and cost nothing. Furthermore, it was situated right next to one of the most memorable buildings in the city, and possibly its most famous church, the Cathedral of St. John the Divine.

Charles had started going to church at St. John while he was living in the Towers Nursing Home. And in the same way he met Marie Drew by coincidence, he met the man in charge of the cathedral. Charles says it's his personality that "usually gets me things," but it is also his up-front manner that attracts people's attention, not to mention the fact that he dresses in a Stetson and black leather boots, the epitome of the urban cowboy, who also happens to be African American.

A chance discussion with the dean of St. John, James Parks Morton, about an etching by the Austrian artist Ernst Fuchs led to Charles being given a place in one of the smaller chapels to keep his easel and drawings.

"It was like my own studio."

In 1979, Morton became the driving force behind efforts to complete the cathedral, whose cornerstone had been laid in 1892 although construction came to a virtual halt after the Depression. Morton had the master builder James Baimbridge brought over from England, where he'd worked on the Liverpool Cathedral, and a man named Chris Hannaway was put in charge of the day-to-day operations of the project and the stonemasons.

"He was a father to me," Charles says of Hannaway. "Anytime I brought something back to church"—meaning stones, of course—"he would give me a place to stash it. He looked after me. The cathedral was like my backyard."

Charles wasn't a stonemason at the time (he would train as one in later years), but he was allowed to use the yard for storage and the church's crane to offload whatever he brought in. He had the kind of freedom that he would never experience again, and he reminisces about those days as if he had been a modern knight-errant going out to save castles on the verge of collapse.

"I was free to go out into the world, and if anything was being torn down I would conquer it and bring it back."

Only after he'd moved the stones from Bedford-Stuyvesant to the Bronx and then to their fifth home, in Williamsburg, did Charles realize how fortunate he had been at St. John. The cathedral was fewer than ten blocks from where he lived, he paid nothing for storage, and he had access to the church crane.

"I was lucky I started collecting when I did."

Each move after St. John got more arduous. The collection was growing in size and, as a result, was more difficult to move. Charles isn't like Nelson, who can build a room for his collection, or Iver, who can rent some storage units. The stones needed lots of open space in a city where land was growing more coveted by developers and less accessible or affordable to a stone-collecting person like Charles.

"I have to go where the space allows it," he says. "I can't just go to some backyard. And the way land gets grabbed in New York, space gets harder to find."

Inevitably, Charles's pastime started costing him money. In Ashland Place, use of the backhoe was free. But in Bedford-Stuyvesant, he had to hire a crane and pay property taxes, however nominal they were. In the Bronx, his fourth location, he had to take out a lease on the land. In Williamsburg, he needed to hire a crane for a week.

In addition to the practical and financial obstacles, there

was often a psychological one. Once he had found a suitable spot, even if it was a dilapidated bank or a piece of ground that wasn't being used, he often had to explain to the land-lord that his stones weren't just tons of unsightly rubble that he was going to offload on the property. Charles had much loftier goals in mind.

"I had to become a master at convincing people," he says. "I'd say to the owner, 'Hey, mister, you're not using the prop-erty. You need someone there. I'll look out for you.'" Part of Charles's argument was that he could help improve the neigh-borhood by bringing in his stones. "I was willing to do some-thing with a space that no one else had the opportunity to do. And that's why I was good for a neighborhood. I wasn't rich, but I would come in and use the stones to enhance the place, take care of it. What I did was something to be proud of."

When the bank in Bedford-Stuyvesant was sold, Charles found an abandoned building in the Bronx, formerly the Bronx Borough Courthouse, that he thought would be perfect for the stones. He put his case to the borough president, Fernando Ferrer, and eventually got a lease on the paved section of a small triangular block at the intersection of 161st Street and Third Avenue. But it was probably the building on the other half of the block that drew Charles's attention in the first place. It was just his style: gorgeous and heartbreakingly in need of attention.

The 1914 Beaux Arts structure had been empty since the 1970s, and even though its colossal Tuscan columns, vous-soirs, and archivolts were intact and unscathed, the windows were bricked up and graffiti rose seven feet high on the walls. Lucky for the goddess of justice above the entrance, she had been just too high to reach.

To Charles the courthouse was a "little island," and for the first time at a location in New York he began to place the stones in some kind of order. When he was still in Brooklyn, opposite BAM, he noticed after the stones had been deposited how they unintentionally formed a kind of façade. The arrangement in the Bronx, meanwhile, was more deliberate. Atop two granite bases on the front steps, from which bronze lampposts had once protruded, he put cornerstones, and on each of them went a capital.

"The stones were gorgeous," he recalls. "It looked like the ruins of Rome."

Charles refers to the courthouse several times as the ruins of Rome, giving a sense of romance to a structure that was, in fact, forlorn and defaced. Like his talk about valiantly conquering buildings, and architects who were "masters," and the Towers Nursing Home being a castle, and the destruction of "a holy empire" at Mt. Sinai, his words have the effect of recalling a time long ago, when buildings were more important than they are today. They were the result of craftsmanship, heavy stones, and time-consuming labor.

In 1996, when the courthouse was put up for auction, Charles had to gather his stones and move once more. The borough president's office had in any case been trying to force him to leave, because his promise to turn the island into something for the community hadn't happened, and most of the stones, mahogany ties, and gates just stood there and gathered dust and graffiti. Instead of uplifting the neighborhood, the stones merely added to the sense of decay.

Charles would come a lot closer to fulfilling his dream at his next site, on Kent Street, in Williamsburg. Kent Street might not have had all the amenities of St. John, nor was it as cheap, but it did offer the best location by far for his collection—half a block of open ground on the bank of the East River, right across from downtown Manhattan. The single leftover building on the land, the Brooklyn Eastern District Terminal warehouse, wasn't well-known but it added a nice nineteenth-century touch.

"I at last had enough land to do whatever I wanted," Charles says. "There were guys coming in by helicopter and boat to see this property, but the owner let me have it. That was pretty nice."

On Kent Street, Charles created what he considers his best work, a much larger and more striking version of the Palm Beach garden made of sidewalk paving and old fireplaces. For a week he had a man bring in his crane to help him move the stones around.

"It's like creating an installation. You have to think where the stones will look best. You don't just stack them. You want it to be pleasing so that it will involve people's minds."

A series of pieces were strung along the edge of the lot closest to Kent Street. Near the entrance, several flat stones were brought together to create what Charles calls an altar. At its center was a cornerstone from P.S. 64, and on top of that went the lion from St. Alphonso's. When someone told him that the book that lay open between the lion's front paws represented the beginning of the New Testament, "the altar" truly gained a biblical significance. For Charles, the setting itself was even more significant: Behind the stones, across the East River, was the world's most famous skyline.

"You could see history, and then Manhattan in the back of the stones. Even though the stones were taken down"—which is a kinder way of saying they came from a demolition—"you saw what went into making something great. This was a part of the city that no longer existed. So here you had something valuable against a valuable landscape. I wasn't trying to sell anything. I was giving you history. It was like a cemetery of New York. And for people it was like a sanctuary."

Charles says the stones changed Kent Street while they were there. Tour buses used to make a detour to see this odd arrangement, and an impromptu art exhibition was held on the grounds. Twenty artists came together and created installations that somehow reflected and added to the spirit of the stones, whether it was by wrapping trees, making dogs out of wire to put on the roof of the old warehouse, or decorating the concrete stumps of a factory that used to be there. None of this would have happened without the stones, and in Charles's view that meant they helped bring a moribund piece of land to life.

"It kind of gave a composition to the waterfront, which was so untamed."

Whatever good Charles thought he might have been doing on Kent Street, he was, paradoxically, regarded by locals as a harbinger of change. A man who wanted to bring back the past was misidentified as someone who was presaging the future. He was also an easy target, or at least his stones were, being left unguarded as they were for long stretches of time. "I was seen as a developer. And I stood out like a sore thumb." Kids regularly used to jump the fence and scribble graffiti on the stones, and one day they got into the warehouse and set fire to the flammable part of the collection Charles stored there. His days on the river, he could see, were numbered.

Then, in 2000, seven blocks of property on the East River were sold, including the half block Charles was using. So he had to move again. By now he had accumulated more stones, and to transport them to their next home he needed five forty-five-foot trailers, each of which had a capacity of ninety thousand pounds. Charles was the owner of two hundred tons of old New York.

The day I meet Charles outside the refectory of St. Patrick's, he is easy to spot in the hustle-bustle of Midtown. Even though he's dressed in the right color, black, he stands out from the people rushing to lunch or a business meeting. He wears lace-up boots, tight pants over slightly bowed legs, a jacket with decorative braid that makes it look like part of a naval uniform, and a Stetson with a wide brim. Slung around his neck is a Leica, and there are two more cameras in a black bag hanging from his shoulder.

He has an ageless face, and he looks and sounds more like a student of twenty-one than a man thirty years older. His conversation is peppered with phrases that sound like they were once hip. "That blows me away," he will say, or he'll use words like *slick* and *wicked* to signal his approval of something.

We are on our way to visit his five-trailer, two-hundred-ton collection, which is now being kept at his latest location, his eighth in New York. Unbeknownst to me, it is also the least remarkable and, quite possibly, the saddest, for everything about it signals the end for Charles's stones. They are gradually being pushed to the sidelines, unwanted and unappreciated.

At St. John, Charles was at the center of things; in the Bronx, he was moved a bit farther uptown; in Williamsburg, he had to go across the river; and now, way out in east

Brooklyn, he is literally on the periphery. At the same time, his hobby has never cost him more. His monthly rent for the latest property is equal to what he paid for an entire year at the Bedford-Stuyvesant bank. After more than two decades of transplanting the collection from one part of the city to another, finding a worthy home for it, piling it up, unloading it, you can hear the exhaustion in his voice.

"It's a hassle to find the space, to move. For me to house the stones and keep them, I have to *be* that person. If I had a place of my own, I'd be like a runaway train. But when you always have to move them, they're never settled. I don't want to be a slave to a stone, always having to come back, build it up and take it down. That takes a lot out of you. My mother says that if I had put my energy into one building rather than into many, I would have a very beautiful building somewhere."

At the same time his artwork, the career he was following before he left Palm Beach, has suffered too.

"I sometimes feel that if I'd done my drawing [all this time], I could've afforded to buy a mansion, not just gotten the stones."

The Sisyphean challenges make him waver, but he never gives in. One moment he will say, "I've gone through this collecting phase. I need to get on with my life." The next moment he will qualify himself: "If I do collect another building, it'll be because it's a landmark, it's coming down, and I should try and save it." Ultimately, he admits that he can't ever give up collecting. "It's in my blood."

He even manages to work up some excitement about the property in east Brooklyn, although there are numerous reasons to be disillusioned.

"It's like a hideout," he says excitedly, referring to it every now and then as "Jesse James country."

To get to Jesse James country, we have to take a long subway ride and then an equally long bus ride past warehouses and then a cemetery. It looks nothing like Jesse James country outside the window, dull and gray and industrial, but I know that isn't what Charles had in mind. He was talking about the spirit of the place. Nor is it a coincidence that Steven, the book collector, also used the analogy of the Wild West. "I think people that collect would have been cowboys or something like that," he told me. "They can't be tied down." Scott, meanwhile, said collectors reminded him of the daring forty-niners of the gold rush, and Dave the sludger brought up "Crocodile" Dundee. Whether cowboy, prospector, knight-errant, or train-jumping circus performer, in the end the ultimate quest of every collector seems to be, at least in part, freedom and adventure.

We are the last passengers on the bus, and the road gets narrower until we drive along what could pass for a country lane, except for the fact that it is bordered on one side by a wall and, beyond that, one of the busiest thoroughfares in the city—the Long Island Expressway.

When we walk from the bus stop, it starts raining. Three dogs Charles adopted from a local shelter are meant to be protecting his property, although when we get there they look less ferocious than miserable. The somber mood is only heightened by the presence of a derelict house next door and the smoky, noisy blur of traffic on the LIE. At that point there is little doubt that Charles's collection has been moved to a kind of urban twilight zone. In spirit at least, the city whose architectural history he is trying to preserve couldn't be more distant.

All of Charles's stones, besides a few columns he is still allowed to keep at St. John the Divine, are squeezed onto the small lot. The five trailers are parked side by side and are piled high with, among other things, door frames; capitals; granite columns; doors; sculptures; cornerstones; a granite Star of David; a massive rock from a park that was being excavated; a gigantic wooden hen; countless railroad ties; fourteen gates, several of which came from a nineteenth-century meathouse in the Bronx; and a huge bell-shaped piece of wood that was once used to cast ship propellers.

To the left of the trailers stand five fire engines: a Diamond T fire engine and pumper, a C Grade 100-foot straight-ladder truck, a Mac diesel truck, an America la France pumper truck, and an army tank retriever truck. Between them are the relics of two old Chevy pickups, and the body of a 1929 Plymouth. Some of the vehicles are burned black along their flanks, the more obvious victims of the arson in Williamsburg, although all of them are in an equally bad state of repair.

Unlike the stones, the fire engines and trucks weren't found. Charles paid for every one of them, although to him there is no difference between old things that are bought or found.

"I love history," he says. "I have always loved the past. I know the materials were better and they would last longer."

One fire engine, the 1948 C Grade, came from the Scarsdale Fire Department, and he saw it on sale when he was going to visit his mother in Queens one Sunday. He knew that if he didn't buy it, "it would land up in some South American country," and in some curious way he believes that the vehicle is better off serving out its time on a lot next to the LIE unused but saved.

When we leave Jesse James country, the place seems sadder than ever, as if the stones will never be arranged again like they were in Williamsburg, that their fate from now on is to

be stuck on the back of this quintet of trailers, in disarray and
forever on the lam. But I am wrong. Several months later,
Charles will move the stones to a better site, this time in Red
Hook. There will be striking similarities to Williamsburg, not
only because the suburb is an up-and-coming enclave of warehouses that are being transformed into business and lofts, but
also because the stones will once again be on the water. And
the view across the top of them will be of another famous
part of the city's skyline: the Statue of Liberty.

When Charles and I walk from St. Patrick's to the subway to
go to Queens, the route he chooses seems arbitrary. He takes
photographs along the way, and I assume that our route has
something to do with what he's shooting. But before I know
it, we have covered twenty blocks and are standing at the
corner of Thirty-third Street and Eighth Avenue. Right in front
of us is Madison Square Garden, the monstrosity that was
built on the site of the old Penn Station after it was torn down
in 1964.

"Look at that versus that," says Charles, pointing to the
featureless façade and then, on the other side of Eighth Avenue,
to the old James A. Farley Post Office. The gracious Beaux
Arts building and the destroyed railway station were designed
by the same firm of architects at the beginning of the twentieth century, and it was the station's demolition that gave rise
to a greater awareness among the public of the value of old
buildings and made life a bit harder for anyone who wanted
to knock them down.

Charles doesn't have a piece of the old station, for its destruction predated his collection by a decade, but, as always, he
finds a way of figuring himself into its story, the same way

that he did by living in the Chelsea Hotel and collecting door-knobs from the Towers Nursing Home. In this case, the connection is even more tenuous. His small removal company has, on several occasions, helped move equipment for the son of Senator Daniel Moynihan, who until his death was an advocate for re-creating Penn Station in the post office. You can tell from the way he talks about Moynihan that he saw him as a fellow knight-errant, fighting for the holiest of empires.

As we continue walking, Charles snaps the post office, or rather, Penn-Station-to-be. Mostly he shoots with the Leica, but occasionally he pulls out his Nikon too. All the cameras are old, of course, although his passion for photography is new. It has also had a quite unexpected outcome, for it is where his collecting has been able to accommodate his art, or vice versa. He takes pictures of buildings, on top of which he superimposes shots of objects that figure prominently in his life: crosses ("Jesus is always in my photos"), women ("She was from Brittany. I shot through her hair. She blew me away"), and fire engines. They too are collections of a sort.

"If I walked past a building being torn down now," he says, "I would shoot it and collect it."

The last time I see Charles, in fact, after he has moved to the new location in Red Hook, he is photographing two buildings that were destroyed only a few days earlier. The structures have fallen not because of an act of demolition, however, but because of an act of terror. He spends entire days at Ground Zero, recording the devastation caused by the attack on the World Trade Center.

Once again, as with Marie Drew and the dean of St. John, he has met the right person at the right time, and he's been given access to the site, or rather, to a building next door.

"I started talking to this lawyer who took me to his office and let me use the fire escape. I stay there all day and shoot."

In each photo, Ground Zero is in the back, the cranes and bulldozers unmistakable, but superimposed on it are more colorful images and people. And as always, Jesus is there, this time represented by an Infant Jesus of Prague statue that Charles picked up out of the trash. Tragedy behind, hope in front, and God always present.

Witnessing the catastrophe daily has made a deep impression on Charles. Like countless other people he is talking about the creation of a memorial to the buildings and the victims, but he has a different take on what it should be and where it should go. For Charles, the ideal place to put a monument would be at the very top of the unfinished Gothic cathedral, St. John the Divine. You would have one piece of modern New York architecture now gone, one piece of old New York architecture still going up. The idea of marrying the two landmarks may seem outrageous, but coming from a collector of pieces of the city, whether lost, discarded, or forgotten, it somehow makes sense.

acknowledgments

Without collectors, there wouldn't be a *Mongo*. They spoke to me unreservedly and colorfully, and whether they take up a chapter or a sentence—or don't even get mentioned—they all helped me immeasurably. And I thank them for that. In particular, I would like to single out Dave, or, as he likes to call himself, "Dave Sludge," for having been so enthusiastic, phoning me up with regular updates on his discoveries, or, more typically, the lack of them. Joe Monkman, Elaine Buchsbaum, and John Ferrone encouraged me throughout the writing of *Mongo*, and helped me to find some of my best collectors. Without their help and faith in me, this would be half a book. Luke Janklow, my agent, stood behind my decisions, and Gillian Blake at Bloomsbury always pushed me in the right direction. This is as much their work as mine.

a note on the author

Ted Botha was born in New York and grew up in Japan, South Africa, and Washington, D.C. He has written for numerous publications, including the *New York Times*, the *Los Angeles Times*, the *Wall Street Journal*, *Condé Nast Traveler*, and *Outside*. His first book, *Apartheid in My Rucksack*, was a personal account of discovering Africa as a white African.

a note on the type

The text of this book is set in Linotype Sabon, named after the type founder, Jacques Sabon. It was designed by Jan Tschichold and jointly developed by Linotype, Monotype, and Stempel, in response to a need for a typeface to be available in identical form for mechanical hot metal composition and hand composition using foundry type. Tschichold based his design for Sabon roman on a font engraved by Garamond, and Sabon italic on a font by Granjon. It was first used in 1966 and has proved an enduring modern classic.